NORTH STAR

A Drama in Two Acts
by
GLORIA BOND CLUNIE

Dramatic Publishing
Woodstock, Illinois • London, England • Melbourne, Australia

IMPORTANT BILLING AND CREDIT REQUIREMENTS

All producers of the Play *must* give credit to the Author(s) of the Play in all programs distributed in connection with performances of the Play and in all instances in which the title of the Play appears for purposes of advertising, publicizing or otherwise exploiting the Play and/or a production. The name of the Author(s) *must* also appear on a separate line, on which no other name appears, immediately following the title, and *must* appear in size of type not less than fifty percent the size of the title type. *On all programs this notice should appear:*

ACKNOWLEDGMENTS

I am very grateful to the many people who have helped bring *NORTH STAR* to life. Many thanks to the National Endowment for the Arts, The Getty Center for Education in the Arts, and the Council for Basic Education for the initial grant; Columbia College Theatre Music Center, Chuck Smith and the Theodore Ward Prize for African-American Plays for mounting the first workshop; and Dennis Zacek, Sandy Shinner and Victory Gardens Theatre for mounting the first professional production.

NORTH STAR received its premiere in 1995 at Chicago's Victory Gardens Theatre.

NORTH STAR

A Drama in Two Acts
For 5 Women and 7 Men (6 with doubling)

CHARACTERS

AURELIA TAYLOR . . . . . . adult Relia, African-American

RELIA TAYLOR . . . . child Aurelia, Negro, 11

MANSON TAYLOR . . . . Relia's father, Negro,
thoughtful, determined undertaker

KATE TAYLOR. . . . . Aurelia's mother, Negro,
loving but "does not play"

WILLIE JOE POOLE. . . . . best friend of Relia, Negro, 12

MISS COOPER . . . . the librarian, white

GRANMA. . . . . Manson's mother, Negro

FRANKLIN. . . . . community college student, Negro

HAWKINS . . . . friend of Manson, Negro,
janitor, big talker, but dedicated to "the cause"

REVEREND BLAKE. . . . . family minister, Negro,
friend of Manson's, soft-spoken, clear-sighted,
slight stutter, quiet will of steel

MR. CONNELL . . . manager of five and dime store, white

JAKE. . . . . a farmer, white
(can be played by Mr. Connell)

VOICE OF UNCLE FRANK. . . . . Willie's uncle,
killed but appears in a dream. (played in silhouette by
Franklin or other male character)

THE TIME: Present day and the summer of 1960.

THE PLACE: A large northern city
and a small town in North Carolina.

ACT ONE

SCENE ONE

SETTING: *A beach in a modern northern city. Summer. Night.*

AT RISE: *A silhouette of a mother and child are seen. The child sings "This Little Light of Mine" joyously. [NOTE: Actor who plays RELIA would be child in silhouette. AURELIA is the mother of this child.] Indistinct whispering voices begin ... They get meaner. Child sings softly, bravely, but her voice cracks. Whispers end in audible, angry whisper.*

VOICES. Nigger... *(Child stops singing.)*

(In the dark, faint, late-night city-sounds, traffic almost in slow motion. AURELIA TAYLOR rushes to the beach. The sky is full of stars. She covers her eyes as if looking for something behind her eyelids. She opens her eyes and looks up again at the sky, angry and frustrated.)

AURELIA. I can't believe... I can't believe he called my daughter... That cab driver called my baby girl... It was under his breath, but she heard it. A whisper, but in the dark it echoed down the street like cold wind on a mission... And she heard it. I saw it in her eyes and she sees in mine... She sees in mine... I didn't know what

9

to do. I grabbed her hand and walked away ... ran away. I avoid her eyes now. She's frightened because I'm frightened. It rattled something deep. Something I'd put away a long time ago. She's waiting. What do I say?

I don't want her to fear ...

I don't want her to hurt ...

I don't want her to know ...

God, why couldn't I have stopped it!

(AURELIA has flashback from the past. She hears/sees GRANMA singing "I've Been 'Buked and I've Been Scorned." Then AURELIA hears/sees MOTHER singing part of "Ain't Gonna Let Nobody Turn Me 'Round." Song stops when scene begins.)

RELIA. Ow ...

KATE. Hold still ...

RELIA. Ow ... Mommmmmyyyyy ...

KATE. Told you a million times ... Now, you all banged up ... scarred ...

AURELIA *(trying to touch memory)*. Mama?

RELIA. You're the one ... says pretty on the inside ...

KATE. When it starts to heal ... we'll put cocoa butter on it. And leave the scab alone! *(Lights fade on RELIA and KATE. AURELIA does not want them to fade away.)*

AURELIA. I don't have a bandage for this one, Mama. No cocoa butter. I can't remember how to make it heal ... I can't remember how you ... Where do I find ...? They told me a million times ... in a million ways ... but what did they say? *(KATE's voice singing softly ... AURELIA watches RELIA, the child version of herself, sneak out-*

side to escape bedtime. She sneaks up on MANSON, covers his eyes.)

RELIA *(to MANSON).* Shhhhhh ... *(They laugh and become quiet conspirators in the night.)*

(RELIA and MANSON sit on the front porch steps of their two-story home in the Negro section of a small southern town. They live beside the funeral parlor MANSON runs. It is a night in 1960. Sometimes AURELIA interacts with her memories, at other times she observes. She desperately wants to be a part of these moments in the past.)

MANSON. Humpty-dumpty back together again? *(RELIA holds wound up to be kissed.)*

KATE *(inside house).* Manson, is Relia out there?

RELIA. Shhhhh ...

MANSON. Be in in a minute ... *(MANSON looks up.)* Do you see it?

RELIA *(shakes head).* I can't find it.

MANSON. Shhhhhhh ... Close your eyes. *(RELIA closes, then opens eyes. Lights dim or go to darkness.)* It's so dark ...

AURELIA *(doesn't close eyes).* Daddy ...

MANSON. Girl big as you, still scared of the dark. Close your eyes. Good. Now, count to a hundred.

RELIA *(opens eyes).* A hundred?

MANSON. No peeking! Count!

RELIA/AURELIA *(with eyes closed).* 1, 2, 3 ... *(AURELIA opens eyes, RELIA continues to count slowly.)*

AURELIA.
Daddy, I can't... I can't find
the stars anymore...

The sky's so different now. So
small...
I've lost them.
Too much light from build-
ings, cars...
Not like before...

When I was a girl in Caro-
lina,
We had big skies! Huge skies!
With millions and millions of
stars.
Brilliant stars in black night
skies,
That made you look up and
wonder!
Held you in reverence.
Demanded you see them!
Made you accountable for tak-
ing up space under their
brightness!
Ohhh, to turn off city lights
and to see those stars again!

MANSON (to RELIA).
Slow down...

That's better...
Much better...

RELIA.
99, 100.

MANSON. Now... Open!

(The sky is now a country sky, darker and filled with
stars.)

RELIA (uncovers eyes). Wow! They changed!

AURELIA. So much brighter!

MANSON. No, your eyes just got used to the dark ...

RELIA (*staring at the sky*). Where do you think they come from?

MANSON. God blinked and there they were...

RELIA. Wouldn't you be scared, sittin' way out there in all that darkness?

MANSON. Not if I was a ball of light.

RELIA. Wonder how many there are?

MANSON. Lord, if questions were money, child...

RELIA. How many?

AURELIA. How many, Daddy?

MANSON. Billions!

RELIA/AURELIA. Billions?

KATE (*calling from inside*). Relia... Relia, why are you still out there? It's past your bedtime.

MANSON. Be in shortly...

Is this about stars or stalling?

RELIA. You been out here every night this week.

MANSON. Got a lot to think about...

RELIA. 'Bout the sit-ins? Are you worried about the sit-ins? I'm not worried about the sit-ins. I can't wait to have my turn! Well, maybe a little bit worried... You worried about the sit-ins, Daddy?

MANSON (*pause*). You know, the stars are a lot like people. Not what they seem, at all. Giant balls of energy reduced in our minds to tiny pinpoints of light. All the same, yet all different. All sitting in one sky. (*Pause.*) I reckon we'll do all right... Just got to remember...we're in the company of stars.

RELIA. Mama wouldn't call them all stars... She called some of them redneck...

MANSON. Relia!

RELIA. She said it!

MANSON. Once! And don't you ever repeat...

RELIA. But...

MANSON. End it!

RELIA. Mama says she's not sure I should demonstrate. You wouldn't let her stop me, would you? I've got to be there!

MANSON. White stars, blue stars, new stars, novas... I'll talk to her. *(Pointing stars out to RELIA.)* That group is the Kite of Hercules and over there is the Northern Crown... *(Pretending to take crown from the sky and placing it on RELIA's head.)* For my lady!

RELIA. Ohhhhhh!

AURELIA. Thank you!

RELIA. What's your favorite?

MANSON *(pause)*. Granpa favored the North Star.

RELIA. Granpa was blind.

MANSON. Could still see the stars. Said the North Star was his star, so I guess it's my star, too.

RELIA. Sounds funny. Like you could put it in a will or something.

MANSON. Maybe, not in a will, exactly...

RELIA. Never can find it by myself.

MANSON. Right at the end of the Little Dipper...

RELIA *(pointing)*. There?

MANSON. Not enough stars...

RELIA. There?

MANSON. If you were Harriet Tubman, we'd all speak Spanish, now. First, close your eyes. *(RELIA does so.)* See it inside. Seven stars... a bowl with a handle. Got it?

RELIA. Yes!

MANSON. Now, look!

RELIA *(opens eyes).* There?

MANSON. Close. That's the Big Dipper. The two bright stars on the outside of the bowl? They ... *point* to the North Star. The faint stars, that's the Little Dipper. Big Dipper, Pointer Stars, Little Dipper ... North Star ...

RELIA. Big Dipper, Pointer Stars, Little Dipper ... North Star! I see it ... I see it! *(Pointing to stars as she finds them.)*

MANSON. Now, you're Harriet Tubman, freedom bound.

RELIA. ... freedom bound!

MANSON. Tie a string to the North Star. Pull down, just like you're pulling a shade. Now, put your nose right on the string and you're facing due North ... and this way is ...

RELIA. South?

MANSON. And this is ...

RELIA. East ...

MANSON. And this is ...

RELIA. West!

MANSON. Now hug the one that you love best! *(RELIA hugs MANSON, who spins her so she sees North Star.)*

RELIA. I see it! I see it! Gotcha, North Star!

MANSON. Now, find it again. *(RELIA and AURELIA turn around. MANSON spins RELIA fast until she is dizzy and laughing. When RELIA and AURELIA stop, neither can find the North Star.)*

RELIA. It's gone!

MANSON. No, you just got turned around. When you need it, close your eyes, and look here first *(Points to heart.)*

RELIA. I'll never find it on my own!

MANSON. Yes, you will, and then it'll be your star, too.

(KATE enters drying a dish.)

KATE. Manson, that child needs to go to bed.

MANSON. We're moving in that direction, now.

KATE. Not unless she's sleeping in the garden!

RELIA *(to MANSON)*. Ah, come on, it's not like I've got school or nothin' ...

KATE. Anything ... school or anything ... and summer or no ... you still have to be up early, young lady. You're supposed to make signs over at the church at nine o'clock.

MANSON. A few more minutes won't hurt her ...

KATE. All right, you two. Manson, I'm putting you in the waking-up department tomorrow. Let's see you tangle with Miss Stargazer then.

MANSON. You know something, I think it's time for bed.

KATE. Chicken!

RELIA. Daddy?

MANSON. You heard your mother! *(AURELIA heads upstairs.)*

KATE. Go on. Clean pajamas on your pillow. And let that scab be. Needs time to heal, for goodness sakes.

MANSON *(hugging KATE)*. You just want to be alone with me on a starlit night.

KATE. Only if you want to be alone with me ... and these dishes.

MANSON. Sounds interesting! *(They kiss.)*

RELIA *(shouting from upstairs window)*. These are too little!

KATE. Then stop growing and get some out of your bottom drawer.

RELIA. I don't see any in the bottom drawer!

KATE. Aurelia Katherine Taylor, find something, say your prayers and be in that bed before I get upstairs, or I will be on you like thunder followin' lightnin'.

MANSON. How about being on me like thunder following lighting.

KATE *(smiling and hugging)*. Man, you are worse than she is. Come on in. You haven't even eaten yet.

MANSON. Can't. Got a few last-minute things to tie up on the Wilson funeral, then I promised to run over and help Ms. Edwards pick out a suit for John. She's taking his death so hard.

KATE. You coming right back?

MANSON. Well, I need to meet with Brother Green and the Rev...

KATE. Another meeting? Morning... midnight... mass meetings... meetings before you meet...

MANSON. I'll grab something later...

KATE. We haven't sat down to a meal together in I don't know how long.

MANSON. You think we're gonna eat our way to freedom?

KATE. If you drop dead before we get there, it won't mean a whole lot, will it?

MANSON. Well, when you get to heaven, you can tell me about it.

KATE. How? You're not going to heaven!

MANSON. I'll see you later.

KATE. At least go up and kiss Relia good night. Before you know it, she'll be at Granny's.

MANSON. Yeah, about Momma's... Listen, Kate, it won't kill anybody for her to go at the end of the summer, will

it? She and her friends have their hearts set on demonstrating...

(RELIA enters quietly and listens.)

KATE. That's exactly why I want her at Mama's. These
kids think we're playing. Things get serious... I'd rather
her be down there. That way, we can focus on what
we've got to do.

RELIA. Ahhh, Mommy.

KATE. Girl, you better get in bed and stop eavesdroppin'
on grown folk conversation.

RELIA. I'll miss everything!

KATE. There'll be plenty to do when you get back.

RELIA. But, Mom...

KATE. Girl, we've been fighting for freedom three hundred years, we won't wrap up the battle in one summer.

RELIA. But, Willie, all my friends...

KATE. I hope they're good letter writers!

RELIA. Daddy, I promised...

MANSON *(to AURELIA)*. We'll talk in the morning.

RELIA. But...

MANSON. In the morning... *(AURELIA exits.)* Kate... I
think she should stay.

KATE. She's too young!

MANSON. No, she's not.

KATE *(shouting up to RELIA and avoiding MANSON's
concern)*. In bed, Aurelia, and turn off those lights. Do
you think we have a dynamo in the backyard! An
eleven-year-old child, still sleeping with the light on.
She'll be in college afraid of the dark.

MANSON. Listen...

KATE. Manson... I don't know. But right now, let me see
if I can get this child in bed before the sun comes up.

MANSON. Kate...

KATE. Manson... It doesn't always do to see things too
early. I'll have to think about it. Aurelia! The light!

*(KATE enters house, MANSON watches the skies for a
minute longer.)*

AURELIA. My mother didn't play. There was a right way
and a wrong way to everything according to her. It was
her job to make sure the way I found was always the
right way. If I strayed, she was pretty quick to help me
find the path again. Things weren't quite so black and
white with my dad. He was like reading a good book,
you didn't always understand. I watched him watch the
skies, standing still as pond water on a hot summer day.
Lately, since the sit-ins, he'd been watching the sky a
lot. Standing outside for hours then going off to another
midnight meeting.

*(MANSON goes into house just as HAWKINS enters,
rushing up to the porch. He is nervous and out of
breath.)*

HAWKINS. Manson, Manson... Glad, I caught ya... Willie
Joe Poole's been arrested.

MANSON. What?

HAWKINS. Four white boys jumped him after the demonstration. I'm not quite sure what started it, but...

MANSON. What's he charged with?

HAWKINS. Disturbin' the peace.

(KATE comes out on porch.)

KATE. Manson?

HAWKINS. Evenin', Kate.

KATE. What's wrong?

MANSON. Willie Joe got beat up and arrested.

KATE. Is he hurt bad?

HAWKINS. Don't know. Nobody's seen him. His mama was too scared to go down to the jail, so she run got the Reverend. Reverend called me, say pick up Manson and meet him down there. We got to get that boy out to-night!

MANSON. OK. Calm down...

KATE. Lord, Relia would go crazy if anything happened to Willie...

MANSON. Kate, just to be on the safe side... you and Relia sleep downstairs till I get back. But hold off telling her anything till we get more news.

KATE. You think it's that bad?

MANSON *(goes down steps, then comes back)*. I'll be back when I can.

KATE *(whispering)*. Manson. Why do you have to go? Let them handle it.

MANSON. Kate, I've got to. If we don't do something quick... you know, they're liable to slip that boy into some creek and we'll never hear of him again. It'll be all right.

KATE. You can't promise me that. You keep going out in the night and I keep wondering are they gonna slip you into some creek.

MANSON. I'll be back. Now, get some sleep.

KATE. Call me!

MANSON. Don't worry... I'll be back when I can...
(MANSON and HAWKINS exit.)
KATE. Call me!...

SCENE TWO

(Lights indicate we have flashed back to another day. AURELIA sits on porch steps and remembers WILLIE. RELIA shouts for WILLIE. She is not aware AURELIA is there.)

AURELIA. We were all shocked and frightened the night Willie Joe was arrested.
RELIA. Willie Joe!
AURELIA. You see, despite his sorry homelife, Willie Joe Poole wasn't really a troublemaker...
RELIA. Willie! Willie Joe... Come on!

(WILLIE races up to RELIA.)

RELIA. Willie! You've been fighting again!
WILLIE. Some cracker wanted to know why a "little coon" was carrying such a "big book." I just gave him an answer.
RELIA. Willie!?!
AURELIA. Willie just believed in standing his ground!
WILLIE. He started it!
AURELIA. Sometimes I wish I was like Willie, but then again...
RELIA. You gonna get yourself killed one day!
WILLIE. Before I do, you wanna take a look at this?

RELIA. You got it!

WILLIE. I got it! *(WILLIE teases RELIA with the book, playing a chase game, then sits beside her on the porch steps but won't let her see it.)*

AURELIA. He could set a twinkle in your eye, even when you were bound and determined to be mad at him. *(AURELIA's presence recedes as RELIA and WILLIE explore the book.)*

RELIA. Come on... Let me see... Stop being so hateful, Willie. You promised to show me if you found it.

WILLIE. All right, all right! *(Getting serious.)* Now, I'll show you, but then you got to keep it to yourself. If your daddy found out, he'd kill us both. Spit swear!

RELIA. Nooooo... We're too big for that stuff.

WILLIE *(will not give her the book).* Spit swear!

RELIA. I hate this, this is so nasty. Spitting is so nasty.

WILLIE. You want to see it or not?

RELIA. You just make me do it because you know I hate spitting in my hands. Ohhhhh. All right. *(WILLIE and RELIA perform a swearing ritual they have done since they were small. Both rub the ground, spit on their hands, rub their palms together, then shake hands.)*

RELIA/WILLIE. Spit swear! While we both walk the face of the earth, I promise never to tell!

WILLIE. Now wipe your hands real good! *(WILLIE wipes his hands on RELIA's clothes, then shows RELIA the book. She is amazed as she turns pages. AURELIA watches.)*

AURELIA. But even as he laughed and joked, you knew Willie's sense of adventure marked him as sure as a cracked egg loses its insides.

RELIA. Where'd you get this?

WILLIE. I hatched it!

AURELIA. His quick mind or his quick mouth could lead him into the shadow of death...just like his Uncle Frank.

WILLIE *(to RELIA)*. Close your mouth and stop eatin' flies, girl!

AURELIA. Maybe he joked so much 'cause he didn't want folks standing around expecting his funeral.

RELIA *(scrutinizing the page)*. You sure it goes like that?

WILLIE. It's plain as day, with pictures and everything!

RELIA. Looks uncomfortable.

WILLIE. According to my brother, you get used to it and it's kinda nice.

RELIA. Has he done it before?

WILLIE. Says he has...lots of times.

RELIA. But he's not even married!

WILLIE. You don't have to be married.

RELIA. Mama says...

WILLIE. Well, girls do, but boys don't.

RELIA. That doesn't make any sense. Who do they do it with?

WILLIE. Girls who *aren't* gonna get married. Girls like the ones on Green Street, or the ones boys talk about when they're hanging over car engines and grinning...

RELIA. Have you ever done it. *(Long pause.)*

WILLIE. Never found a girl I really wanted to do it with. One worth holding onto. Like Uncle Frank used to say, "Don't want myself tied down to some little nobody, with small ideas and no sense." You could have a baby doing this. Wouldn't want the mother of my children no less brilliant than me.

RELIA. Swear truth?

WILLIE *(long pause)*. Truth? Scared to ask the girls that would and wouldn't ask the girls I know. They're more just the kissing kind. You ever been kissed before, Relia?

RELIA. You?

WILLIE. I asked first.

RELIA. Not really.

WILLIE. Ever wonder what it's like?

RELIA. Hmmmmmmmm.

WILLIE. I could show you?

RELIA. You mean on the lips?

WILLIE. No, on your knee! Yes, on the lips.

RELIA. Does that mean we're going steady?

WILLIE. Heck no. Let's just call it an... an experiment.

RELIA. Should I shut my eyes?

WILLIE *(looks at book and then at RELIA)*. Don't have to...

RELIA. Uggggh... Close your mouth.

WILLIE. But the book...

RELIA. The heck with the book. I don't want you spitting all over me!

WILLIE. OK... OK... At least pucker up! *(WILLIE/RELIA kiss, seriously at first, but then they're not sure how to end it and WILLIE starts laughing.)*

RELIA. Stop laughing!

WILLIE. I'm sorry. You want to do it, again?

RELIA. No!

WILLIE. Sure?

RELIA *(shakes head no)*. You play too much.

WILLIE *(referring to book)*. I was just...

RELIA. Where'd you get this, anyway?

WILLIE *(makes a big deal out of showing her the spine of the book)*. The back room... *(Whispering.)* in the library.

RELIA. That's no big deal... I been to the library before! Haven't seen a book this nice there, though. Why, it's almost new!

WILLIE. I don't mean the *colored* branch... I mean the big one, with the huge columns out front...

RELIA. You got this from the white library?

WILLIE. Couldn't get books this nice in the colored library!

RELIA. How in the world...?

WILLIE. You wanna go?

RELIA. It's getting late.

WILLIE. Not much past four.

RELIA. Mama would kill me!

WILLIE. Chicken!

RELIA. I can roast your rooster any day!

WILLIE. Then come on... and I'll show you the *real* library! Here, hide this! (*WILLIE hands RELIA the book. She hides it under the porch. AURELIA takes it out and looks at it. WILLIE and RELIA head for the library. RELIA is somewhat awed by the outside of the building.*) Come on! (*RELIA hesitates.*) Come on, will ya!

(*WILLIE enters with confidence, RELIA enters reluctantly. WILLIE drops his head as he approaches the scrutiny of the pale-faced LIBRARIAN. RELIA drops her head.*)

WILLIE. My daddy's sick, this gal's gonna help me.

MISS COOPER. That's fine, Willie. And, Willie, what I tell you about comin' in the front door?

WILLIE. Just forgot, ma'am.

AURELIA. Granma always said...

(*GRANMA appears.*)

GRANMA Don't want no grandbaby of mine prancin' through no back doors. Can't go in the front... don't go.

AURELIA. Willie grabbed my arm and led me into the storage room. Started handing me dust cloths and a broom.

RELIA. What?

AURELIA. He grabbed a bucket and a pail.

WILLIE. Come on.

RELIA. Willie?

AURELIA. I was so dumbfounded, I didn't know what to do but follow him... Granma's voice ringing in my head... *(WILLIE pushes her down on her knees and he starts cleaning.)*

GRANMA. Girl, I don't want you cleaning up behind no white folks. Get your education and don't bring no report cards with mess on 'em. I want A's and maybe, just maybe, since the Lord is the only perfect being, on occasion a B... with a plus (+) behind it, mind you. You smart. You smart girl. You can do and be anything you want, child. Just get your education. Don't want you end up cleaning in Miss Ann's kitchen.

AURELIA. When I asked her...

RELIA. Did you ever clean in Miss Ann's kitchen?

AURELIA. She was silent for a long time.

GRANMA. Only when my children were hungry... or needed books... But I don worked too hard to ever see you on your knees, child.

RELIA *(holding cloth and wondering what to do)*. Willie?

WILLIE *(pulls RELIA back onto her knees)*. Shhhhhh... start cleaning.

GRANMA. Lord, have mercy! *(GRANMA exits.)*

AURELIA. Hmmmmmmm. It was quiet as a tomb and almost as empty as we dusted table after table.

MISS COOPER. Willie? When you're done, child, pull the door to, the lock's already on. Hope your father's feeling better soon. See you tomorrow.

WILLIE. Yes, ma'am. *(MISS COOPER exits. WILLIE jumps on table and shouts.)* Welcome to my world! You in high-cotton, now, girl! What you wanna read?

RELIA. Can we do this?

WILLIE. We're doing it!

RELIA. But are we free to...

WILLIE. Free? Free! Heck, Relia, Uncle Frank used to say, "It's the *little freedoms* we *take* that'll keep us sane till the big freedoms come."

RELIA. I'm scared...

WILLIE. Why?

RELIA. I don't know, but it doesn't feel right.

WILLIE. Girl, I used to think so too! But look around! Why not! It's a public library! Makes me feel like when Uncle Frank used to fly me. Pick me up, hold me over his head and fly me like I was on top of the world! Come on, Relia, fly! Fly with me? Grab a little freedom and fly!

RELIA. I'm not so sure...but...

AURELIA. There were wonders there you wouldn't believe!

RELIA. Amazing things! A globe as big as our kitchen table. Along the walls near the ceiling, plaster pictures of Greek and Roman stories. A rack with more magazines than I knew existed.

AURELIA. I couldn't find *Ebony* or *Jet*, but there were...

RELIA. *Better Homes and Gardens, Highlights for Children*...

AURELIA. ...and a whole slew of them I'd never seen!

WILLIE. What you want to read about?

RELIA. Gosh, I don't know... Ahhh... The stars... I want a book about the stars!

AURELIA. He took me to a place that had row after row of books on...

RELIA. ...the stars... the moon... the universe! *(RELIA softly reads from a book about the stars and the constellations as AURELIA remembers the library.)*

AURELIA. This became our place. Willie's and mine. We wandered through the aisles, surveying the world... Mostly the white world, with an occasional volume by...

RELIA. Booker T. Washington...

AURELIA. ...or some such passive soul. Willie felt free to borrow one or two to take home. I don't know what the soft-voiced librarian did if someone else requested the borrowed volumes, but she never said anything to Willie or me when we came to clean. *(AURELIA turns pages from the book the children had earlier.)* Only occasionally, when Willie's father wasn't too drunk, did he bother to come with us. And when he did, Willie still handled most of the cleaning... with his father slowly turning pages and looking very sad. We began to stay later and later. Sometimes Willie would leave a back window open, walk me home and then come back to finish the cleaning. One day, we were reading this great book about Greek mythology...

RELIA. Zeus!

WILLIE. Hera...

AURELIA. ...and matching the stories to the pictures on the wall.

RELIA. Prometheus!

AURELIA. When before we knew it...

RELIA. Oh my word, it's an hour and a half past supper-time! My folks are gonna kill me!

(They run to RELIA's porch. KATE and MANSON are waiting. KATE is furious. MANSON is quiet. KATE fusses at the speed of light! She does not stop to let them explain.)

KATE. Where in the world have you two been?

RELIA/WILLIE. We were...

KATE. Whatever you've got to say, I don't want to hear it! It's almost two hours past supper! We were half crazy with worry. Where in the world could your head be that you didn't realize it's two hours past supper?

RELIA/WILLIE *(try to explain)*. We...

KATE. Don't even act like you have anything to say that will make good sense! The least you could have done was call instead of having us call all over town, worried sick, worrying the neighborhood... Why in God's name didn't you call? *(WILLIE and RELIA try to answer.)* And don't tell me you didn't have a dime to call! If you don't have a dime in your shoe to call when you leave, then you don't have any business stepping off this front porch! Give you a little freedom and what do you do with it? I've always thought of you as a young lady with good sense... We raised you as a young lady with good sense... Didn't we raise you with good sense? You better answer me when I ask you a question. Didn't we raise you with good sense?

RELIA *(confused about how much to say)*. Yes, ma'am...

KATE. And you, Willie, I know you got good sense!

WILLIE *(quickly)*. Yes, ma'am.

KATE. I depend on your good sense when this child's good sense goes out the window! Where was your good sense tonight? *(WILLIE tries to answer.)* Don't even talk to me! Go home, see your mother so she can finish fussing at you. Go on! Now! *(WILLIE and RELIA exchange looks. WILLIE exits, running.)* Your father said, "Kate, she's got good sense," and I was fool enough to believe him. Should I have been fool enough to believe him? *(RELIA tries to answer.)* Girl, don't you even talk to me! Don't even talk to me! You better talk to this girl, Manson... Talk to your daughter, because I'm so angry, if I *listen* to her anymore, I might just go crazy and kill your child! *(Pause. In the silence, RELIA turns to MANSON.)*

MANSON *(quietly)*. I'm disappointed in you, daughter.

AURELIA. For a girl, the disappointment of a father is like reaching to the bottom of a well when you're three days thirsty—and finding sand.

MANSON. Where have you been?

RELIA. At the library with Willie.

AURELIA. He got even quieter.

MANSON. Daughter, you can die and go to heaven or you can die and go to hell. That will be your choice based on the way you live your life, but don't ever lie to me. Library's only open Tuesdays and Thursdays and Saturdays.

RELIA. I wasn't at the *colored* library, I was at the *white* library...

MANSON. YOU WERE WHERE?

KATE. What? *(Pause.)*

AURELIA. When my father cooled off...

MANSON. What in the world?

AURELIA. ...and this took a considerable time...

MANSON. Where in God's name...

AURELIA. After he cooled off...

MANSON. What possessed you...

AURELIA. ...he heard all about our voyages.

RELIA. More books than you've ever seen! *(RELIA gives MANSON book from library.)*

MANSON. Books, huh...

RELIA. ...and a globe...a globe... *(RELIA shows him the size of the globe.)*

MANSON. A globe...huh...

RELIA. ...bigger than the kitchen table! And all along the walls...paintings and...

MANSON *(to KATE)*. You know, in forty years, I've never seen the inside of that library.

KATE. Foolish and dangerous.

AURELIA. He seemed to regard me with newfound respect.

MANSON. Gotta hand it to 'em, Kate. You ever read a book from there? They got spunk, all right!

KATE. Just plain crazy! Both of you are just plain crazy! Relia, go to bed!

RELIA. Mama... *(RELIA exits to bedroom. KATE and MANSON argue as they exit.)*

KATE. And you standing there encouraging her...

MANSON. They're just children, Kate... Gotta spread their wings... When I was...

AURELIA. Though it took some doing, our library adventures continued. I guess Daddy understood about taking *little freedoms*...till the *big freedom* comes.

(RELIA enters and curls up in bed with a blanket and a book.)

AURELIA. He began to supplement our reading with the
likes of Frederick Douglas and Langston Hughes, Arna
Bontemps and Zora Neal Hurston... Books he would get
when he drove to Detroit to buy a new hearse or go to a
black embalmers' convention in some northern city.

*(KATE comes upstairs, turns off RELIA's light, RELIA
turns on flashlight. MANSON enters, signals her not to
tell and turns on RELIA's light again. RELIA turns off
flashlight and falls asleep.)*

AURELIA. Years later, after seeing the glories of big city
public libraries, I came back to that place of forbidden
fruits with its fading globe and well-thumbed volumes on
the universe. It looked like a small room with books in it... a
small room with a big sky. God, where did that sky go?

SCENE THREE

*(Later, the evening of WILLIE's arrest. KATE enters,
guiding a sleepy RELIA into the living room.)*

KATE. Come on, Relia.
RELIA. What time is it?
KATE. Late.
RELIA. I smell coffee.
KATE. Your daddy wants you to sleep downstairs tonight.
RELIA. Why?
KATE. Don't worry about "why," just come on. You can
snuggle up on the sofa until he gets back.

RELIA. What's wrong? Where's Daddy?

KATE. He went with Hawkins to meet the Reverend. Now you know almost as much as I do, so no more questions. Good night. (KATE turns off light.)

RELIA. Mommy! (KATE turns on a small, dim light then exits.)

AURELIA. The night Willie was arrested, I really needed the light. I used to get so scared sometimes, when Daddy was away. It was weird. I felt like I had a hole in my stomach. A dark hole that I couldn't fill up with anything. Like I was homesick, even though I was home. I'd felt it before and Daddy told me ...

(MANSON enters, cradles RELIA as if she's a small child.)

MANSON. Oh, that's just the growing-up-hole! You have to have a place to store all the stuff you need to learn and feel to grow up. And it's bottomless ... like a black hole.

RELIA. Is it dark inside? You know I'm scared of the dark. Is it dark?

MANSON. Very dark ... until you see ...

RELIA. What? What will I see?

MANSON. Look real carefully, and way near the end-that-doesn't-end, you'll see a light! And staring back in that light is an older person, that looks like you.

RELIA. Looks like me?

MANSON. Looking at you! That's why it's called the "growing-up hole."

RELIA. But why does it hurt so bad?

MANSON. Sometimes, right about the time you're ready to do a whole lot of growing, you can feel it getting bigger. Stretching... It hurts a little bit but then, you just start filling it up with good growing-up stuff... Good thoughts, things you've done well... And you hardly notice it's there.

AURELIA. Does it ever fill up?

MANSON. I hope not!

AURELIA. Not even when you're an old, old lady?

MANSON. Not even then. You just have to know what it is, so you're not afraid when you feel it. *(MANSON exits. AURELIA tries to follow, but he is gone.)*

AURELIA. I can still feel it, Daddy... Daddy... I want... I want the hole filled up... I want...

SCENE FOUR

(No actual scene break. AURELIA, hearing MR. CONNELL, turns and is in the LIBRARY. CONNELL is a pot-bellied, middle-aged store manager. His "I want" should immediately echo AURELIA's "I want.")

MR. CONNELL. I want the Raleigh paper, if that's not too much trouble.

MISS COOPER. Not at all, Mr. Connell.

(MR. CONNELL sits to read the paper. WILLIE enters.)

MISS COOPER. In early, aren't you, Willie?

WILLIE. Records day for colored teachers. Half day at school. Thought I'd finish up before it got late, if that's all right?

MISS COOPER. Not many folks here, I don't think that'll be a problem. Go 'head.

(RELIA enters nodding.)

RELIA. Ma'am. *(RELIA and WILLIE begin to clean the library. They move about MR. CONNELL, dusting and sweeping. CONNELL moves automatically, without being aware they are there, as he reads the paper. It is like a dance between two people who can't acknowledge the other.)*

MR. CONNELL *(responds to news article, without noticing children).* Coons! *(RELIA and WILLIE are offended and angry, but must keep cleaning.)*

AURELIA. It's interesting to watch a world when that world isn't aware that you exist. Especially, if being aware of their world is so important to your survival. You appear and disappear when needed, and otherwise, go unnoticed.

MR. CONNELL *(crosses to MISS COOPER's desk with paper in hand).* You going to the church supper tonight?

MISS COOPER. I might be? How's your sister feeling?

MR. CONNELL. Oh, she's still pretty poorly. Just can't seem to shake those allergies. Goes outside the house, and you think she was watering the grass the way her eyes tear up.

MISS COOPER. I would go to the church supper tonight, if I had a ride I could count on. My ole car is trying to act up and sure wouldn't want to be stuck out with it at night. But it seems so late to call anybody.

MR. CONNELL. Oh, now, you know I wouldn't mind picking you up atall. Wouldn't mind atall. I'll holler at home, then be by 'bout seven if that's OK.

MISS COOPER. Why, that would be mighty kind of you, Mr. Connell.

MR. CONNELL. Then I'll see you 'bout seven. Shoot, I better get outta here and pick up some gas. Wouldn't wanta run out drivin' you home, now, would I?

MISS COOPER. I don't know about that... Where you been burning up so much gas?

MR. CONNELL. Oh, here and there. Took a day and ran over to see my cousin in Winston-Salem. Stopped in Greensboro. *(CONNELL and COOPER freeze each time AURE-LIA speaks. RELIA and WILLIE continue cleaning.)*

AURELIA. You are aware and don't even realize you are aware of everything they do and say.

MISS COOPER. Greensboro? What's new in Greensboro?

AURELIA. You are aware you go unnoticed, and some-times you begin not to notice how unnoticed you are un-til something jars you into their conscience. *(WILLIE drops book or mop. CONNELL notices briefly and con-tinues.)*

MR. CONNELL. Lord, they got some mess going on downtown there! Ever since those colored kids started that sit-down mess, don't know whether you can find a decent place to eat or not downtown. Sitting in Wool-worth's talking about they want to be served. Shoot, if they were really hungry, there's a stand-up counter not fifteen feet away.

MISS COOPER. I know, I know...

MR. CONNELL. Tell ya, some of the businesses just closed up the eating sections. Just took the chairs out rather than have niggers dictate what was gonna happen in a store we done owned longer than they been black! It's not just in Greensboro, seem like every little town and crossin' trying some kind of mess. It's all in the paper here. Spreading like the jitterbug. Only it's the Niggerbug. Lord, I hope we don't see that mess over here. Not at my lunch counter. If we're not careful, we're going to have niggers everywhere!

MISS COOPER. Our Negroes aren't that big 'a fools. It's just those college kids not knowing what to do with themselves come summer.

MR. CONNELL. Maybe so, maybe so. But we got to keep an eye out. Shoot, look at the time. Let me get out of here. I pick you up at seven.

MISS COOPER. See you later! *(As MR. CONNELL exits, he and RELIA briefly look at each other, he sees her for the first time. COOPER puts away a book and goes to get purse. WILLIE pretends to put up paper CONNELL has left, but is really trying to read it.)*

WILLIE *(head in paper).* Greensboro is still at it! Been demonstrating over four months! *(WILLIE hides paper behind him as MISS COOPER returns.)*

MISS COOPER. Willie, I'm locking up just a little early, today. I doubt anybody's going to drop in this near closing.

WILLIE. Yes, ma'am.

MISS COOPER. Pull the door tight when you finish. Hope your father feels better. *(MISS COOPER exits. WILLIE reads paper.)*

RELIA. Come on, Willie Joe. Let's get this done first, then we can read.

WILLIE. Seems like every town in the state has had some kind of sit-in... Raleigh, Durham, Statesville, even Monroe... Everywhere 'cept us.

RELIA. As many late-night meetings as Daddy been to, we may be having one soon. Been over to Winston-Salem and Roxboro and to Greensboro twice. There was a big old meeting over in Raleigh where Dr. King spoke and everything. When he's not out of town meeting, he's at a church or the barber shop or the funeral parlor with a group of folks. When they're not meeting...

SCENE FIVE

(No actual scene break. Manson's home or funeral parlor. Eight p.m.—Civil Rights Planning Meeting. RELIA and WILLIE help KATE and MANSON, HAWKINS, FRANKLIN, and REVEREND set up furniture for meeting. A burst of loud argument as they enter. They freeze mid-argument.)

RELIA. They're meeting about meeting... *(Another loud burst, RELIA to MANSON who is in the midst of meeting.)* Can we stay?

WILLIE. Can we?

MANSON. If I don't hear a peep!

KATE. Manson...?

MANSON. Children got to learn sometimes. Willie, call your mother, tell her you'll be late... *(Burst of argument about future demonstrations. ALL freeze except RELIA,*

MANSON and AURELIA.) Real late...but I'll bring you
home.

RELIA. What are you doing at all these meetings?

MANSON. Organizing!

RELIA. Organizing what?

MANSON. People, baby.

RELIA. How? *(Burst of very angry sound from middle of
meeting. MANSON stands among frozen people, talking
to RELIA.)*

MANSON *(smiles to himself)*. Patiently.

AURELIA. But I have no more patience... How...? *(AURE-
LIA, moves among and points to frozen people as if nam-
ing stars.)*

MANSON.	AURELIA.
It's like learning the stars... Each one is different... Each one, a whole solar system with its own peculiar planets. So many ideas of how things could be. It all has to fit into some Grand Design. Organizing people is like trying to figure out what that mysterious Grand Design is...	Orion Ursa Major Ursa Minor Big Dipper Little Dipper Pointer Stars Polaris!

*(AURELIA points to MANSON on Polaris. She becomes
a silent player in the meeting. There is a burst of angry
sound. Freeze.)*

MANSON. Before they kill each other! *(Meeting continues,
ALL talking. FRANKLIN and HAWKINS are in midst of
argument.)* I can't hear! I can't hear! Franklin has the floor!

(FRANKLIN has been trying to convince MANSON, KATE, HAWKINS, and the REVEREND to begin demonstrations against the downtown merchants. They have been arguing a long time; it is now almost 2:00 a.m. They are tired, but still arguing with vigor. WILLIE and RELIA are in the corner, falling asleep. FRANKLIN argues with HAWKINS.)

FRANKLIN. Now, I don't mean any disrespect, sir, but I don't want to be as old as you before I can sit at a lunch counter downtown and get myself a meal. Matter of fact, I don't want to be as old as you before I can work in one of those stores that don't seem to have any problem taking my money. For that matter, I don't want to be ancient before I can buy a store on Main Street, so I can take their money!

HAWKINS. You're not gonna change things, in a day or two, that were here long before you knew what a diaper was, boy!

REVEREND. Look at Montgomery, man. It took them a year just to get the buses desegregated.

FRANKLIN. But, if we don't start... We've got students ready now! I say we go ahead.

HAWKINS. I don't see why we're fooling with these kids...

KATE. Because nobody needs to go off half-cocked in all different directions.

HAWKINS. We don't have a jack-bird's chance your way. I say talk first, then pull out the big guns if they're not listening.

FRANKLIN *(shouting)*. Listening? So, all of a sudden, they're gonna listen? Man, we gotta ride the momentum of Greensboro... *(FRANKLIN takes paper WILLIE has brought from library.)*

HAWKINS. Boy...

FRANKLIN. You had fifty years to do it *your* way. Now, it's *our* turn!

HAWKINS. And I'm supposed to roll over and pretend it doesn't matter if it gets done right?

FRANKLIN. Gets done right? Lord, is that what we've been waiting on all these centuries, to do it right?

HAWKINS. Be careful, boy.

FRANKLIN. I just want to get it done!

HAWKINS. How you get it done is important! If I'm hungry, I can steal a loaf of bread or I can work for it.

FRANKLIN. Ahhhh... Massa... Masssssaaaa. Massa. I so sorry I ain't worked hard enough! Gimme a few crumbs, massa, pleasssssseeee.

HAWKINS. Get out of my face, boy!

MANSON. Both of you, that's enough...

FRANKLIN. Everybody else been eating off this lousy loaf of bread, how come we can't get some?

HAWKINS. If you're not careful, bread can lose its flavor!

FRANKLIN. Hell, If I don't taste it, the flavor won't matter!

REVEREND. All jackasses and mules...just...hush! *(Everybody stops, stunned.)* Stop butting heads and let's see if we can get something c-constructive done. It's getting late, and I don't mean clock time.

KATE. Oh, Lord, it's past two...

MANSON. Let's decide something! I've got a funeral first thing in the morning.

KATE. So...what do we do? And don't anybody else raise their voice in my house, again! *(Pause.)*

FRANKLIN. I'm sorry. *(Pause.)* Just give us a chance. That's all we're asking. *(Pause.)*

RELIA *(gets paper, hands to MANSON)*. Daddy, paper says, everybody's demonstrating... *(Pause.)*

MANSON. It couldn't make matters much worse... Kate?

KATE. We got to make a move sometime.

MANSON. Reverend?

REVEREND. As I said, it's getting late...

MANSON. Hawkins?

HAWKINS. I still don't know... but I guess I'll go along with Kate and the Reverend.

MANSON *(to FRANKLIN)*. We're talking about only four or five students to begin with... with backup in the store, of course. Just test out the situation... See what happens...

REVEREND. Like a trial balloon...

MANSON. Then, we'll approach the mayor with our demands...

KATE. Here's the final list...

MANSON. Good... good... desegregate lunch counters, black clerks... include the *public library* in that.

HAWKINS *(taking list from KATE)*. Yeah... we gonna bust it all out. Lord knows the police and fire department need some color... right on down to the garbage workers... Hell, we pay their salaries.

REVEREND. So when we gonna run this by folks?

MANSON. Monday?

HAWKINS. Flyers be ready tomorrow!

REVEREND. Announcements will be in church bulletins, Sunday. We've got to make sure large groups are ready to go when these white folks say no to our demands.

HAWKINS. Ye of little faith!

REVEREND. Oh, I have faith, I'm just not a fool!

FRANKLIN. Looks like we're moving...

HAWKINS (to FRANKLIN). We may be creaking, but when we cracking, watch out! Hot damn. It'll be just like the voter registration drive in '48. We turned this county out! You kids weren't even wiping your nose good...

MANSON. We weren't even wiping our noses good...

HAWKINS. But it was a hell of a victory, hell of a victory. Went from 8,000 colored voters to 44,000 in less than a year. I was janitor over at the old elementary school. Used to go in... 4:00 in the morning, crank that mimeo up and baby, this here arm could pump out 2-3,000 flyers before the teachers got in.

FRANKLIN. We got electric ones over at the college, now.

HAWKINS. Well, we did it by hand back then.

REVEREND. I hear the P-Presbyterians have a new one, too. Lord, those were some days! We must have sat in every little church this side of heaven.

HAWKINS. Scared them crackers to death!

MANSON. Shoot, scared some of us to death.

HAWKINS. And old "meek and mild" here, put the fear of God in 'em!

FRANKLIN. You threatened people?

REVEREND. Naw. We'd just go pay 'em a visit.

HAWKINS. There were some so terrified to register, when we came to the front door... they'd be sneaking out the back! Well, the Reverend here would ease on round the back and meet 'em. He'd be so gentle-like, they were ashamed of themselves. He'd sit down with 'em and explain how he was "once afraid, but with the Lord's help, he found the strength... "

REVEREND. It's true!

MANSON. They didn't have the heart to say no to his face, and they didn't have the nerve to lie to him! If "meek and mild" Reverend Blake could do it, they sure could! It was perfect!

HAWKINS. Next election, the black vote was so strong, all them crackers were sitting up, paying attention! Mayor Crawford even kissed a black baby...

MANSON. Won the election for him! Asked Mary Phillips would she vote for him and she stuck that baby, dirty diaper and all, right in his face.

HAWKINS. He liked to died, but he kissed it! *(ALL laughing.)* Shoot, one of these days, we gonna get our own man in.

REVEREND. Mayor Manson... sounds good to me.

HAWKINS. But till then, that turkey, Mayor Crawford, better cackle in our key, or he knows his ass is out of there... baby-kissing or not. *(ALL laugh. HAWKINS takes out a small flask.)* To the good old days! Reverend, it ain't going to hurt you none to have a little sip.

REVEREND. It's so late, I think I'll rely on j-just the *holy* spirit for now.

HAWKINS. Suit yourself... *(MANSON subtly signals HAWKINS to put up flask because of children.)*

KATE. Sounds like we're set!

REVEREND. Yes...

FRANKLIN. We're ready!

HAWKINS. And if they don't respond, we'll have the whole damn community eatin' chitlins at their precious lunch counter.

REVEREND. Yes, got to go the distance.

MANSON. Well, we got more than a notion...so come on...let's get a motion. *(ALL form circle for closing prayer. They sing "Oh, Lord, Hold My Hand, While I Run This Race..." as REVEREND prays.)*

REVEREND. Oh, Lord, show our hearts the way and guide our feet as we move on up to victory. *(Singing continues as chairs are removed and WILLIE and RELIA take places. RELIA finishes song as...)*

SCENE SIX

(Street. RELIA AND WILLIE pass out flyers. RELIA has just given someone a flyer.)

RELIA. Come to the meeting. There's going to be a workshop on nonviolence, too... OK? It's real important.

WILLIE. Seems like I've passed out a thousand of these.

FRANKLIN *(holding stack of flyers, runs to catch RELIA and WILLIE)*. Wait up! Glad I caught you. We just got some more printed. Can you guys take Chestnut and Rock Spring first thing in the morning?

RELIA. Sure! Sure!

FRANKLIN. Great! Hurry and finish up here, then head home before your mother gets worried. See you later!

WILLIE *(under breath)*. I hope not!

RELIA. Come on, Willie!

WILLIE. I got to take a break!

RELIA. A short one! It's almost dark. *(Pause.)*

WILLIE. So what do you think's gonna happen with all this?

RELIA. I'm not sure. I guess we'll find out at the meeting tomorrow night. You going?

WILLIE. 'Course I'm going. You going?

RELIA. Of course I'm going.

WILLIE. My cousin, over in Nashville, said there are mass meetings there near 'bout every night. Been like that for months. Said that everybody, the college kids, the high school kids, near 'bout the whole town is taking shifts protesting. They go in, sit at a lunch counter, and ask to be served.

RELIA. Anybody ever get served?

WILLIE. Not yet.

RELIA. Wonder how it is? I mean, I've thought about it ... but to actually do it.

WILLIE. She said things were cool for a little while, then some of those crackers started getting mean ... Pouring ketchup and eggs on 'em, throwing bottles and bricks, burning 'em with cigarette butts ...

RELIA. What did they do?

WILLIE. Said they just sat there. That's what you're supposed to do ... Can't hit, can't curse, can't do nothing but sit there and take it ... Supposed to show you're stronger than evil! (Pause.) Do you think you're stronger than evil?

RELIA. I don't know. (Pause.) I don't know if I've ever seen evil real close up. I mean, we talk about it in church, and I guess I've had some pretty mean thoughts sometime ... but evil is heavy-duty stuff. Sometimes in the dark, I think, maybe it's in my room ... That's why, when I'm by myself at night, I got to have some kind of light on ... But I don't know whether it's really there or not anymore.

WILLIE. I've seen it, I've seen it in broad open daylight!

RELIA. I think, if I've come close, my daddy must have stopped it.

WILLIE. But your daddy can't stop this! Not by himself. Yep, they just sit there, stronger than evil. *(Pause.)* You think you could sit there if somebody was burnin' you with a cigarette butt?

RELIA. I don't know. Could you?

WILLIE *(takes out matches).* Give me your hand. *(WILLIE lights a match/lighter. Pulls RELIA's hand toward flame.)*

RELIA. Are you crazy?

WILLIE. Come on. Try it. Don't pull back. *(She thinks about trying, but changes mind.)*

RELIA. No!

WILLIE *(strikes match/lighter).* Let's see if I'm stronger than evil! *(He holds his hand closer and closer until RELIA knocks his hand down.)*

RELIA. That's stupid! Stop it, Willie. Stop it! *(RELIA grabs matches and keeps them from WILLIE.)*

WILLIE *(angrily).* Yeah, we can stop it now, but what about at the sit-in. You think they'll stop just 'cause you say "stop." Stronger than evil... Me, personally, I'd be kicking some behind... Kick evil's behind up one side and down the other...

RELIA. We'll just see when the time comes. So stop acting crazy. We'll be in it soon enough. *(Hesitating.)* At least, I hope it's soon...otherwise I'll be at Granny's.

WILLIE. Granny's? What do you mean, go to Granny's? You can't go to your granny's now! You just can't go!

RELIA. I got to go! I go every summer!

WILLIE. You can't go this summer!

RELIA. What am I gonna do?

WILLIE. Talk to your mother! No! Talk to your dad! Have him talk to your mother! You got to be here! You just got to be here!

RELIA. I tried to talk...

WILLIE. Naw... don't give me that weak-willed, namby-pamby stuff. You're either with me or you're not! I need to know. Are you going to demonstrate when the time comes, or not?

RELIA. Are you?

WILLIE. When the time comes, I'll be right there in the front lines.

RELIA. Then I guess I'll be there, too!

WILLIE. Swear! Spit swear!

WILLIE/RELIA. Spit swear! While we both walk the face of the earth, I promise to be there.

RELIA. If you weren't the closest thing I have to a brother... I swear... *(Wiping off hands.)*

WILLIE. You wanna seal it with a kiss, instead? *(RELIA and WILLIE break out laughing.)*

RELIA. Get out of here!

WILLIE. Kick evil's behind... stronger than evil... yeah! *(WILLIE exits with library props, RELIA has pail.)*

AURELIA *(bits of memory flood her imagination)*. Oh, Lord! To be able to kick evil's behind up one side and down the other! To be stronger than evil again! Come on, Willie! Show me how it's done! Show me something stronger than evil, brighter than darkness... My daughter's waiting...

SCENE SEVEN

(Library, after five. MR. CONNELL enters, speaks to MISS COOPER.)

MR. CONNELL *(angry tone)*. I need to talk with you about something outside.

(MISS COOPER exits with CONNELL. RELIA dusts as she watches for WILLIE. WILLIE enters.)

RELIA. Where have you been? I had to lie like the dickens to get Miss Cooper to wait so you could get in.
WILLIE. Thanks.
RELIA. So, where were you?
WILLIE. Demonstrating!
RELIA. What?
WILLIE. Demonstrating!
RELIA. You're lying.
WILLIE. Well, not exactly. But the college kids started today and I watched the whole thing.
RELIA. Swear!
WILLIE. I swear. *(Fast spit ritual.)* ...Walk...face... earth...there!
RELIA. Nasty... Huhhhh. Really?

(Lights fade up on FRANKLIN as he enters and is shopping. FRANKLIN replays the sit-in, aware of WILLIE but not aware of RELIA's presence.)

WILLIE. I was downtown and saw Franklin and these college guys, all dressed up—suits, ties—looking right seri-

ous-minded... so, I followed them. When they got to
Roses, they all bought something—pencils, paper, tooth-
paste... Then, they thanked the clerk, real polite-like,
and started walking toward the lunch counter. Weren't
many people there, 'cause it was almost two-thirty...
(Pause.)
RELIA. So... what happened?!?
WILLIE. They sat down!

*(FRANKLIN sits as if at the lunch counter. As WILLIE
and FRANKLIN tell the story, they interrelate with imag-
ined characters at the sit-in.)*

RELIA. At the white counter?
WILLIE *(sarcastically)*. There ain't no black counter! At
first, I don't think they wanted me there.
RELIA. I know old man Connell didn't want you there!
WILLIE. No, I mean the college kids. But when they saw I
was a serious-minded fellow, they didn't mind me
watching atall.
RELIA. What happened?
WILLIE. Well, when they sat down, the waitress looked
like a squirrel eating buckshot. She was screaming, "Oh
my, word... my word... my word... " Then Franklin asked
for...
FRANKLIN. A Coca Cola and a hamburger, please.
WILLIE. She dropped a whole glass of soda all over her
white shoes, then whispered, *(As WAITRESS.)* "We don't
serve colored here... " *(As himself.)* ...and then *took off*
like a scared rabbit. She was running so fast... almost
knocked the manager down. Ms Patterson,
RELIA. ...the colored cook?

WILLIE. Yeah...she poked her head out from the kitchen... *(As MS. PATTERSON.)* "What you doing starting all this mess around here? This ain't Greensboro or Raleigh. Go on away from here and stop this foolishness before there's trouble."

FRANKLIN. We don't mean to cause any trouble. I just want a Coca-Cola and a hamburger...please.

WILLIE *(as MS. PATTERSON)*. "Well, go on home and tell your mama to cook you one!" *(As himself.)* Then Ms. Burwell, the other colored cook whispered, *(As MRS. BURWELL.)* "Leave those children alone and get on back here and tend to your business!" *(As himself.)* By *then,* Mr. Connell was out there...

(MR. CONNELL enters.)

MR. CONNELL. I'm sorry, boys, but you know we don't serve colored at this counter.

WILLIE. Connell was as cool as a pig in mud! As if he'd expected us and had practiced what he'd say. Franklin was even cooler...

FRANKLIN. Well, sir, you served us at the check-out counter over there, how come you won't serve us over here? Doesn't seem quite right. If we could be served at one counter, we should be served at all counters.

RELIA. Sounds reasonable to me.

MR. CONNELL. Now, I want to be reasonable. I read the paper and know what's going on here, there, and yonder, but like I said, our policy at this point is not to serve coloreds at this counter. To be blunt...we don't serve nig...

WILLIE (*jumps up, ready to fight CONNELL*). You don't serve who...?

FRANKLIN (*grabs WILLIE, tosses him back; under his breath*). Sit down and shut up!

MR. CONNELL. Now, I'm afraid I'm going to have to just close this here counter right now. You can sit there till hell freezes over if you want to, but the counter is closed. Girls, why don't you just clear up for the day.

FRANKLIN (*leaning towards CONNELL*). Sir, do you intend to close up every day?

MR. CONNELL (*leaning towards FRANKLIN*). We'll just have to see about that, won't we? (*FRANKLIN and CONNELL stare at each other.*)

RELIA. Then what happened?

WILLIE. They sat quietly for about an hour or so and then left. (*FRANKLIN and CONNELL exit.*)

RELIA. So where'd they go?

WILLIE. The college kids are meeting someplace with your dad and the Reverend, but I had to get over here real quick... Hey, girl, they movin'. So, did you ask your mom and dad? Can you stay?

RELIA. I'll be here. Mom had me promise everything including my soul, but I'll be here. To start with I've got to clean my room, weed the garden, clean out the garage and wash down the kitchen walls. When I'm not on the front lines fighting for freedom, I'll be a pure-dee slave for my mother!

WILLIE (*hands RELIA bucket and cloth*). That's OK, Beulah, long as you get to fight!

RELIA. Here, I've got my own cleaning to do. (*RELIA hands bucket and pail back and exits.*)

SCENE EIGHT

(No break between scenes. Library. MR. CONNELL exits, COOPER calls WILLIE to her desk.)

MISS COOPER. Oh, Willie.

WILLIE. Yes, ma'am?

MISS COOPER. Ahhhhh. Willie, you've been doing an excellent job while your father's been sick...

WILLIE. Thank you.

MISS COOPER. But I don't think that we'll need the library cleaned for a while.

WILLIE. Ma'am?

MISS COOPER. What I mean to say...is... It's really your father's job and, ahhhh...since he's not well enough to take care of it...and, well, I hear you're so busy...demonstrating...

WILLIE. I wasn't demonstratin', I was just watchin'. Besides...you said I'm doing an excellent job!

MISS COOPER. I'm sorry, somebody else has been hired to take over... I'm sorry, Willie. If it were up to me... *(WILLIE races out.)* Willie, Willie?

AURELIA. Willie... Oh, Willie. Later that day, Willie was arrested. And that night, we wondered if Daddy would ever come back.

SCENE NINE

(Aurelia's front porch. One-thirty a.m. The night WIL-LIE got arrested. RELIA is curled up on the sofa, asleep. KATE sits on the porch steps watching the dark, intently. She occasionally glances at the night sky. RELIA wakes, comes to the door. They are both worried about MAN-SON.)

RELIA. Daddy back yet?

KATE. No.

RELIA. What time is it?

KATE. Late.

RELIA. What time?

KATE. One-thirty.

RELIA. Is it OK if I sit out here with you?

KATE *(starts to say no, then changes mind).* For a little bit. *(KATE moves over, as RELIA snuggles up to her. RELIA realizes her mother has a pistol in her hand.)*

RELIA. I thought this was supposed to be nonviolent.

KATE. I believe in nonviolence, but until your father gets back, I'll nonviolently sit here with this gun under my apron. When he gets back, I'll put it away and we'll just not tell him. *(Pause.)* Smells like rain. *(Pause.)*

RELIA. The college kids sat in at Woolworth's today. That's three places in one week!

KATE. I guess it'll be in the paper tomorrow.

RELIA. I wish we could've been there.

KATE. We'll go when the phone tree calls.

RELIA. But we could have gone, just to see...

KATE. That's not the plan. We'll go when we're called. Don't need hundreds of people crowding down there today. Besides, we shouldn't even be talking about this now. Loose lips sink ships.

RELIA. What?

KATE. Just something they used to say when I was a child. *(Pause.)* Yep, smells like rain.

RELIA. Why didn't Daddy go? I could see us not being there ... but how come Daddy didn't go ...

KATE. Wasn't his job. What if everybody got arrested? Who would be around to bail folks out?

RELIA. So that's what Daddy's supposed to do?

KATE. Some of what he's supposed to do.

RELIA. I don't think I can wait till we're called. History's just marching on without me! Folks taking a stand! And I'm here just sitting!

KATE. Calm down and lower your voice. *(Pause.)* Tomorrow, after we finish painting picket signs at the church, I've got to help Miss Burton make lunches for the demonstrators. You want to help?

RELIA. I guess that's better than nothing. Seems funny though, to make lunch for people who been sitting at a lunch counter all day. Can we take it to them, too?

KATE. No. They'll go over to Second Baptist to eat.

RELIA *(surprised)*. But they'll lose their seats?

KATE. Another group will slide right in and hold them. *(Phone rings. KATE and RELIA jump.)*

KATE/RELIA. I'll get it!

KATE. Hush, and be quiet ... *(KATE goes to answer phone. AURELIA stays on steps.)* Hello ... No ... No ... All right. Thank you.

RELIA. Well ...

KATE *(returning to porch)*. That was Doc. Wanted to know if your father had gotten back yet. Wanted to

know if we wanted him to come by. I told him no, we
were just fine, and he didn't need to come over. I told
Delia and John we were just fine an hour ago, I told
Andrea we were just fine two hours ago, I told Kate and
Curtis we were just fine three hours ago, and four hours
ago... who was it that called... The next person who
calls better be your father or it won't matter what I've
learned about nonviolence.

*(Sound of MANSON, WILLIE, REVEREND and
HAWKINS coming. KATE raises gun.)*

KATE. Who's there?

MANSON. It's us.

KATE. Thank goodness... *(Hugs MANSON. MANSON and
HAWKINS help WILLIE into the house. WILLIE has
been brutally beaten. His face is badly bruised and swollen. He is limping and holding ice on his face.)*

RELIA/KATE. Oh, my God.

MANSON. Come on in the house, Willie. Honey, get him
some more ice. *(KATE goes for ice.)*

RELIA. What happened?

WILLIE *(speech muffled from swollen lip)*. I'm all right...
I'm all right...

MANSON. Doc says he should be OK when the swelling
goes down.

RELIA. What happened?

(KATE returns with ice in a towel.)

HAWKINS. A group of hoodlums saw him at the sit-in.
They jumped him over by the library.

WILLIE. Four of 'em. I was sitting on the steps. I just wanted to see who got my job.

RELIA. You lost your job?

KATE (putting ice on face). Don't talk, baby.

MANSON. They left him in the street. When he came to, he staggered over to the police station. (Pause.) He tried to take out a warrant for their arrest.

KATE. He tried to do what?

HAWKINS. Take out a warrant for their arrest.

WILLIE. There were four of them, they beat me up... I didn't do anything wrong.

HAWKINS. Not too many grown men would have dared to do what he did. Try to bring a complaint and all, but he was in his rights to do it. Now, there's a whole new pair of pants on this suit!

MANSON. He was very insistent, and when he wouldn't calm down, they arrested him.

KATE. A twelve-year-old boy?

MANSON. They say it was for his own protection until they could get someone to take him home.

WILLIE (very upset). I told them I got rights! They just laughed at me! I got rights. I read it in a book. They can't do this to me! I got rights!

MANSON. And it's true! If we don't make somebody accountable for the violence now, Lord knows what will happen later.

WILLIE. I got...

MANSON. Willie, we'll work it out... Kate, his mother's scared out of her wits. She thought he'd be safer over here.

KATE. That's fine.

WILLIE. I got rights...

HAWKINS. Doc said give him two of these, they'll help him sleep. *(RELIA gets water, WILLIE takes pills.)*

KATE. Are you hungry ... *(WILLIE shakes his head no.)*

MANSON. Then you all get some rest.

KATE. And you?

MANSON. Folks are meeting at the funeral home. We've got to decide how to handle this thing. We've got to phone ...

KATE. Phone calls? It's three o'clock in the morning!

MANSON. It's better for folks to hear about it now ... from us.

HAWKINS. There're already rumors that he's dead.

MANSON. We need to set up a mass meeting tomorrow, so we can give out the details. Any way we look at it, we'll start full-blown demonstrations Monday.

KATE. Manson, I'm not going to get any sleep. Do you want me to help?

MANSON *(pause)*. Thanks! Start the blue and the red phone trees. The list is on the night table ... Oh, call Barb Nash, she's waiting. Tell her to get flyers out for the eleven o'clock services. You kids get some sleep. We'll be right next door if you need us. Kate, if I see the porch light go off ... *(HAWKINS and DOC exit. MANSON is following them.)*

KATE. I know. Manson ... *(MANSON stops.)* I'm driving Relia to her grandmother's first thing in the morning.

RELIA. Mom ... ?

KATE. Should I take Willie with me ... ?

WILLIE. No!

RELIA. If he's not going, I'm not going!

WILLIE. I can't run away!

KATE *(shouting)*. This is not a game! This is not a game! Look at his face! Boy keep going he'll be just like his uncle Frank, hanging from a tree! *(ALL are quiet.)*

MANSON. I'll speak to his mother in the morning. See what she wants him to do. Get some sleep, children.

RELIA. But, Dad, we've got to be here for the demonstration!

MANSON. You heard your mother. Good night, and not another word about it!

KATE. Relia, take Willie up to your room. You can sleep in our room tonight. *(RELIA and WILLIE exit.)*

MANSON *(pulling KATE outside on porch)*. Kate ... I think they should stay.

KATE. Not Relia. Willie's mother can decide for him, but not Relia.

MANSON. Just think about it.

KATE. No.

MANSON. All right, all right, I won't fight you on this, but I want them both at the meeting tomorrow.

KATE. You're using that child, Manson. You are using that child's beat-up face!

MANSON. I want them both at the meeting! If they've got to go, they can go after.

(MANSON exits. WILLIE/RELIA enter Relia's room.)

KATE *(goes to RELIA)*. Relia, I need to run next door to talk to your father about something.

RELIA. Can't you call him?

KATE. No. I'll be right back. Door's locked. You'll be fine, but if you even think something's wrong, blink the porch light.

RELIA. All right, Mama. *(KATE exits.)* You want some more ice?

WILLIE. Uhhhh...uhhhhh

RELIA. You sure?

WILLIE. Don't need no ice...tired... God, I'm tired.

RELIA. It's the medicine. Just let it put you to sleep, Willie.

(WILLIE's dream. WILLIE hears UNCLE FRANK. GRANMA is singing...humming an eerie arrangement of "I've Been 'Buked and I've Been Scorned." They are in silhouette as WILLIE dreams... Shadows emerge...a tree...an ax... [Note: Phrases in brackets can be said by individuals in shadow or as a chorus.])

UNCLE FRANK'S VOICE. Willie...

WILLIE *(drifting off from exhaustion)*. Can't go to sleep. He won't let me sleep.

RELIA. Who...

UNCLE FRANK. Willie...

WILLIE. Can't go to Granny's. He won't let me...

RELIA. Who?

WILLIE. Got to...

RELIA.
Go to sleep...

FRANK.
Willie

WILLIE.
Wasn't gonna be afraid...

RELIA.
Just go to sleep.

Uncle Frank...

I'll be here...

WHISPERS.
Frank Poole...

WILLIE.
Don't go, Uncle Frank!

FRANK.
She was lying in a puddle of blood.

Going for big freedom, boy.

WILLIE.
Big freedom!

FRANK.
Swear! Spit swear!

WHISPERS.
Frank Poole

WILLIE.
Uncle Frank?

Why?

FRANK.
Wanted big freedom.

Justice!

AURELIA.
Folks only whisper about Frank Poole...

When a white man

[loved his mama]

beat his mama

He took plumb crazy

[Frank Poole]

Said he had rights

[And nobody listened...]

RELIA.
Willie?

WILLIE.
I swear!?!

AURELIA.
Took an ax and

Cut that man's head...clean off.

Wanted justice.

Walked through town, with a bloody head

WHISPERS.

Frank Poole

Waiting ...

FRANK.

It hurts so bad to hate this way ... Don't hate this way, Willie.

WILLIE.

Uncle Frank!

I hid under the bed ...

AURELIA.

Sat in Willie's yard, under the sycamore tree.

Strung him up, [Set him on fire]

in the sycamore tree ...

listening to him pop and crackle.

(WILLIE screams. Dream fades. WILLIE wakes hysterical.)

WILLIE. Mama screamed "No" but Daddy dragged me from under the bed and out to the sycamore tree. He made me look. Said, "Boy, got to know, or he'll end up just like his uncle Frank!" He was all burnt up, swinging in the sycamore tree, meat fallin' off and skin smokin' ... He keeps coming back ... Daddy wouldn't listen, nobody would ... so he keeps coming back to me.

FRANK'S VOICE. Don't hate this way, Willie.

RELIA. It's all right, Willie. You just dreaming.

WILLIE. They kept hitting me and hitting me, I thought I would die like Uncle Frank. Relia, I peed on myself I was so scared.

RELIA. It's all right to be scared ...

WILLIE. Not this kinda scared. It's not drunk scared, like Daddy, I'm scared 'cause I wanted to kill 'em. I wanted to kill 'em dead! Every time they hit me, I wanted them to die. If I had the strength... I would have killed them. If I had an ax or a gun or... I would have killed them all! God help me... I would have killed them. For me and for Uncle Frank, too. And it hurts so much to hate this way. Relia... it hurts... and I'm so scared.

RELIA. It's all right... it's all right to be scared... Granny used to say...

(GRANMA enters or appears behind scrim.)

GRANMA. The only way to beat death is to die... And the only way to beat fear... is to be afraid. Once you've tasted it, you'll know how to chew it... and you can learn how to spit it out. *(GRANMA exits.)*

WILLIE. Relia. I'm not going to your granny's. And you can't go either! You promised, Relia.

RELIA. But my mother...

WILLIE. I could do it with you there. Do it the right way.

RELIA. But, I can't...

WILLIE. You swore!

RELIA. But...

WILLIE. It's the big freedom, Relia. You swore. Spit swore.

RELIA. All right, somehow I'll be there.

WILLIE. Spit swear! *(WILLIE spits on hand and holds it up to RELIA to take.)*

WILLIE/RELIA. ... while we both walk the face of the earth... Spit swear.

AURELIA. I step off the curb with my daughter. We get in quickly. The cab driver is surprised. I give him the address. He says "Sorry, I don't know where it is. Get out!" I start to explain...argue...plead... "It's late, my little girl..." but then he called her... I wanted to kill him! And it hurts so bad to hate this way! Show me how to spit it out!

RELIA. My...

AURELIA. daughter's...

KATE. waiting... (*KATE, RELIA and AURELIA echo words from phrase "My daughter's waiting" creating a brief sound chorus. End echo. KATE and GRANMA may be seen or may be only voices.*)

GRANMA. Pick the scab of an unhealed wound, and blood's bound to run red. You can learn how to chew it...and you can learn how to spit it out!

END OF ACT ONE

ACT TWO

SCENE ONE

AT RISE: *AURELIA on the beach beneath the stars, bits of memory flood her imagination.*

AURELIA. We sit for minutes that feel like hours in the dark. My daughter can feel my anger grow. "Let's walk, Mommy... Let's walk..." she pleads. I breath deeply. Then quietly, I take her hand. We get out and start to walk. The cab driver slowly pulls up beside us and rolls down his window. We turn... And then he looks straight in my daughter's eyes and says... *(Pause.)* "Nigger." It's not the first time she's heard the word... but it's the first time she *really* hears it. And her eyes shock wide. I throw my hands in the air... grabbing shattered silence I cannot catch. She's heard it. Now what do I do before he is gone like a thief in the night with her innocence. He slowly pulls away. I begin to... Then she says, "He's just a stupid cab driver, Mommy!" We stand under very faint stars and in each star I see her tear-filled eyes asking "What can we do?"

(Evening. Church basement. Faint voices singing civil-rights songs like "We Shall Not Be Moved" *come from the sanctuary above. FRANKLIN is conducting a nonviolence workshop. HAWKINS pushes KATE from a chair and FRANKLIN instructs her how to fall. REVEREND,*

65

MANSON, RELIA, and WILLIE are watching. The AUDI-ENCE is addressed as if they are in the workshop.)

FRANKLIN *(pushes KATE to the floor).* That's better, Kate. But you're still too stiff. Loosen up!

KATE. I'm trying...

FRANKLIN *(to workshop).* When you're knocked down to the floor, don't tense up...go limp. You'll break less. If they start hitting, cover your head, first. Then, try to get close to someone else... That gives them two people to hit instead of one, which will help distribute the blows a little more.

KATE *(as FRANKLIN helps her up).* God knows we want to distribute those blows!

FRANKLIN. Good! Now, we have time for one more short round. *(To workshop.)* Who's ready? *(WILLIE rises.)* You don't have to do this today, Willie.

WILLIE. I want to.

KATE. Willie? Manson? *(MANSON nods. KATE sits.)*

FRANKLIN. OK, it's your turn, Willie. *(WILLIE limps up.)* So where's your book, unless you knit? Be prepared, people... Freedom might take a while, so bring something to do. And a book is good head protection.

WILLIE. In case of arrest, my cousin in Nashville says girls should have candy bars and clean underwear in their purse.

MANSON. What? Boys don't need clean drawers to be free? *(Laughter breaks the tension.)*

RELIA. Daddy...

FRANKLIN. All right, all right, come on. Now, remember...no matter what we say or do to you, keep your cool. Go ahead, Hawkins.

HAWKINS *(as white STORE MANAGER)*. What you doing here, boy?

WILLIE. I'd liked to be served.

HAWKINS. Oh, would you. And what would you like?

WILLIE *(uncertain and surprised)*. He's not going to ask me that?

FRANKLIN. Who knows? You might be the first!

WILLIE. A hamburger, fries... and a glass of ice water... please.

HAWKINS. Here's your ice water. *(HAWKINS dumps glass of water on his head.)*

WILLIE *(jumping from chair, ready to fight)*. You sorry son-of-a...

FRANKLIN *(pulls WILLIE back in seat)*. That's what you don't do! People have been cursed, beaten and burned... without cracking... And you just let a little glass of ice water defeat you. I think you're stronger than that. Are you stronger than ice water?

WILLIE. But he...

FRANKLIN. Are you stronger than ice water?

WILLIE. I guess so... *(Pause.)* Yes.

FRANKLIN. Good. Go ahead... and don't pull any punches. He needs to do this.

HAWKINS *(directly in WILLIE's face)*. You wanted ice water... You got it! What makes you think I want to serve your nigger baboon ass at my counter? Huhhh... huh? You better go back to Africa and swing in the trees to show you got some sense. Nigger ain't been nothin', Nigger ain't gonna be nothin'! *(HAWKINS, in one ear, continues to bait WILLIE, while FRANKLIN encourages WILLIE (next speech). WILLIE struggles between them.*

We hear voices in the sanctuary singing "Ain't Gonna Let Nobody Turn Me 'Round...")

FRANKLIN. You're tensing up, Willie. Relax, breathe... Blank out everything else. Get some image in your mind and hold onto it. Look, look at this picture. See that little girl... Little Rock. All those crackers behind her... She was scared, but she didn't crack. Kept on walking, kept on going... You got that kind of courage in you? You got to love that son-of-a-gun into seeing how ignorant he is. Never stoop to his level. Climb on up to higher ground... that's what nonviolence is about. You can do it! Climb on up to higher ground. 'Cause if you're not on higher ground, there's no need fighting for the dirt!

HAWKINS.	WILLIE.
Buck faced Niggerrrrrr! Better not go out in the dark... thou preparest a dark nigger. You think we can't see you? You heard of night vision, well we got us some nigger vision. We gonna lynch your black ass tonight!	... green pastures. Yea though I walk through the valley of... the shadow of death... I will fear no evil... comfort me... comfort me... Thou preparest a table... the presence of mine enemies... I shall fear no... no... no... NO!

(WILLIE cracks. Attacks HAWKINS.)

RELIA. Mama!

KATE *(stands)*. Stop it! He's a child! *(Pause. MANSON pulls WILLIE off HAWKINS.)*

WILLIE. It don't make sense. If somebody's coming to lynch me, I don't need to pray, I need a gun or an ax or something to stop them. If they're gonna kill me, why can't I kill them?

FRANKLIN. You gonna kill them all, boy?

MANSON. And even if you do, will it make you right?

REVEREND. Higher ground, boy! Got to work that hate out of you or it'll get you before they do.

MANSON *(watching from the door)*. You OK, Willie? *(WILLIE nods.)* We'd better break it up now and join them upstairs.

FRANKLIN *(arm around WILLIE's shoulder. Softly)*. It's not easy. That's why we're doing this. You OK?

WILLIE. Yeah... Yeah...

HAWKINS. Sorry, kid. You just start to saying those things and...

FRANKLIN *(to HAWKINS)*. No, you were fine, just fine.

SCENE TWO

(Sanctuary of the church. ALL join in "Ain't Gonna Let Nobody Turn Me 'Round..." *Music fades out as REVEREND speaks. The AUDIENCE is addressed as if they are part of the congregation.)*

REVEREND. "Ain't gonna let nobody turn me 'round"... How easily we get turned around sometimes. When we face a Red Sea of d-doubt and despair, oh, to find the strength of ages past. From Exodus, we learn, nobody could hold God's people, when God demanded Pharaoh, to "Let my people go!" Now I don't have the eloquence of a Martin K-King or an Adam Clayton P-Powell... I just have to put it in plain speech. From the d-depths of degradation and segregation, we're going to move on up to higher ground and claim freedom's soil. Gonna say, "Let my people go!" And to make it to higher ground, we must find the strength to go forward in a loving, non-violent, Christian way. We may not win every battle, but as long as we don't lose ourselves in the mire of hatred and anger, the war cannot be lost! Now, Brother Manson will review a plan we feel will help us in our e-efforts. Go 'head, Brother Manson.

MANSON. Thank you, Reverend. While watching our sister cities across the state battle segregation, we have *talked* for a long time about what are we going to do here. Now it's time for action. The Granville College students have tested the waters and found the river of segregation running deep. They demonstrated nonviolently, but the beating of one of our children indicates things have become more serious. On Monday, mass demonstrations and boycotts begin. The phone tree will call and let you know what time you're assigned. Now, I know you have been reading the paper and watching the news, but this sit-in thing can be even harder than it looks. If you're going to demonstrate, sign up for one of the workshops. Saying you're nonviolent is one thing, but being nonviolent is a whole different ball game when somebody's beating you over the head with a baseball bat. Now...

HAWKINS. Brother Manson... I know we've been here for a while, but may I have the floor for a just a minute or two? I'll be brief!

REVEREND. That'll be a miracle!

HAWKINS. There's just one little point that's important we all understand before we leave.

MANSON. Go head, brother.

HAWKINS. Now, people, let me just lay it on the line like laundry in the breeze! See those doors back there? They closed for a reason. And before it's all over, our mouths need to be as closed as those doors. So, if there are any questions, discussions or *objections*, bring it forth tonight! Open up, speak out and air your grievances now, behind the closed doors of the Lord, because when we pass through later on tonight, we got to walk as a unified front. (*Pause. No interruptions.*) Do I hear anybody? Sure? Good! Just so we are clear... Gonna break it down for you one more time. Now I'm not talking about anybody special... But don't want any loose-lipped Uncle Tom's tellin' massa what we doin' down in the slave quarters. I tell you like Harriet Tubman told her passengers; she raised that shotgun of hers when they got scared, or wanted to run back, or didn't know what to do... She said, "Dead folks can't jaybird talk... you keep on going now or die!" We can't have no jaybirds singing like a canary, killing our movement... So if you are Polly parrot, better fly the coop now! In other words, we have agreed...

MANSON. Yes, brother... Stand together and keep our mouths shut!

HAWKINS. That's it! Can't have no backbiting... No backsliding, no contrary walking or two-faced talking! We have agreed...

REVEREND. Stand together and keep our mouths shut! Break it down, brother, break it down!

HAWKINS. Get it clear and straight, or it's got to wait... till we're back together behind the closed doors of the Lord's house! We have agreed ... Let me hear you say it now...

ALL. Stand together and keep our mouths shut! *(Amens.)*

HAWKINS. Again, Louder!

ALL. Stand together and keep our mouths shut!

HAWKINS. After you leave this place, You can take it to the Lord in prayer... but just make sure He's the only one there! In other words we have agreed, so...

ALL. Stand together and keep our mouths shut!

HAWKINS. Keep your ears open all you want, especially at your place of work... but...

ALL. Stand together and KEEP OUR MOUTHS SHUT!

HAWKINS. Thank you. *(HAWKINS sits.)*

MANSON. And you know if Hawkins can keep his mouth shut, there ain't no excuse for anybody else! *(HAWKINS and OTHERS laugh.)* Any more questions? Good. Sign-up sheets for shopping carpools, phone tree calling, lunchmaking and others are in the back.

REVEREND. Praise God. Let us stand. We ask, Lord, that you be with us in our struggles "so can't nobody turn us around." We ask for the strength to overcome nonviolently and we thank you in advance as we claim our victory in your name. Amen. *(The CONGREGATION breaks up. WILLIE is staring at RELIA.)*

KATE. Come on, Aurelia, we've got to get going.

RELIA. Just a minute, Mama... *(KATE leaves WILLIE and RELIA to talk.)*

WILLIE. Relia, you promised.

RELIA. I know... but...

WILLIE. Relia, big freedom's coming and you promised.

KATE. Relia, come on! *(RELIA and KATE exit.)*

AURELIA *(watching the beach sky).* Oh, Lord, deliver us from everything that's evil, and all the days of our lives, may we walk in the light of billions and billions of stars,

as we move on up to higher ground... Forever and ever.
Amen. The cab moves slowly down the street and we
stand in silence under a starless sky. "Mama... Mama...
I think it's going to rain." It's gonna rain...

SCENE THREE

*(Light change to Granma's farm, late morning. GRAN-
MA sits, meticulously balling yarn. She smells the air.)*

GRANMA. Gonna rain.

(KATE and a sullen RELIA enter.)

GRANMA. Willie didn't come?
KATE. No. *(To RELIA.)* Why don't you take your bags in
the house.
RELIA. Please... I'm going to miss everything! *(Exits into
house with suitcase. Pause.)*
GRANMA. Smells like rain.
KATE. She's really bent out of shape about not being
there, but under the circumstances...
GRANMA. What did you expect? Since the day she was
born you been preparing her for something like this. Pre-
tended like it was teaching her history... Wasn't history,
it was future you were teaching her. So why are you
surprised? If you plant a pear tree you better not go
looking for plums in the spring.
KATE. I'll call you.
GRANMA. We'll be fine.

(KATE exits. GRANMA rolls yarn. RELIA enters.)

GRANMA. So, you're going to mope?

RELIA. It's not fair! Willie didn't have to come.

GRANMA. You're not Willie, are you?

RELIA. You have no idea how I feel!

GRANMA *(offers yarn to RELIA who hesitates, then accepts the job).* No idea? Humphhh! No idea... Listen, child, when I was a youngster, to get to school, me and my cousins had to pass by this white school. Now, their school was a nice big, brick building, had green grass growing out front with ivy on the walls, and ours was in an old tobacco barn. Our school bus was made of worn, brown shoe leather, if we were lucky, and was at the bottom of our legs. So when their school bus passed, they spit out the window at us.

RELIA. Ahhh... Nasty!

GRANMA. What was worse, everyday, at this one place, the same group of white kids locked arms. Forced us to walk in the ditch while they walked on the sidewalk. Wet or dry, we were in the ditch. There was this one boy, Connell Willis, and his cousin Avery who was the ringleaders of it all. Foul-mouthed little buggers. Well, this happened day after day, month after month until Reesee, who was a pretty thing, but tall as a boy and twice as strong, got new shoes. New shoes in the middle of the school year! That day, when Connell blocked our path, Reesee jumped him and all we saw was legs and dust... *(Laughs.)* When that dust settled, she was the only one getting up. She beat the tar out of that boy. We were jubilee!

RELIA. Wow!

GRANMA. Well, then, this old white lady lived on the corner came out. Everybody stood dead-still. She said, "I been watching you from that window since September and that boy you just beat the tar out of...is my great-nephew." We were so scared, we could have all peed in unison, right there. Then she said, "I'm so glad you did it, I don't know what to do. He deserved ever' bit of it. Now get up, boy, go wash your face and if you breathe a word of this to your parents, I'll make this whippin' seem like the first course to the main meal." There is a God! From that day on, we didn't have no trouble walking on the sidewalk... Now spit from the bus was another matter...that was a battle of another sort, for another day. But we didn't have no problems with the sidewalk.

RELIA. Wow!

GRANMA (pause). Baby girl, you don't know how badly I wanted to be Reesee that day...but I wasn't. I guess there were plenty of battles I missed, but plenty I fought too. (GRANMA gets up, spits on the ground.)

RELIA. Tomorrow's my battle. I just know it!

GRANMA. Maybe so...maybe no. Just be ready when the lightning strikes, and your day will come!

RELIA. I've got to be there, I promised Willie!

GRANMA. Well, baby girl, unless you plan to walk all the way to the next county, you're gonna be fighting another day. (GRANMA exits.)

AURELIA. The mind of a child can seize upon an unintended idea like dustballs gathering beneath a bed...until, one day, it seems perfectly rational to justify their actions by saying... "But Granma said... I should walk"!

RELIA. I could do it! I could walk! I know the way by heart!

AURELIA (*trying to warn RELIA*). By car...we've only been by car... (*Remembering.*) In the old, black Oldsmobile, my feet barely touching the floor...

RELIA. Won't take much more than an hour...

AURELIA. In a car! (*RELIA hears AURELIA for the first time. She is shocked and then feels a growing pain.*)

RELIA. Owww...my stomach...

AURELIA. I had fallen, headfirst, in a growing-up hole.

RELIA. One deeper and wider than I've ever felt! (*RELIA and AURELIA circle each other. AURELIA begins to cover her face.*)

AURELIA. I don't want you to see... (*RELIA takes her hand down, gently. AURELIA and RELIA look at each other.*) For the first time... When I peeked into the growing-up hole...

RELIA (*quietly amazed, trying to recognize this strange, older image of herself*). I see her...

AURELIA (*quietly amazed*). Like looking in a clouded mirror, there was...

RELIA. ...an older me staring back...

AURELIA. Where did this child go? (*RELIA accepts AURELIA but realizes she must convince this older, more practical AURELIA to go.*)

RELIA. I could do it... It's only three towns away! I could go when Granma's sleeping... I could make it for the demonstration tomorrow.

AURELIA. No!

RELIA. I promised Willie.

AURELIA. I know...but...

RELIA. I'm going!

AURELIA. You don't have to do this...

RELIA. I promised Willie... You coming?

AURELIA *(reluctantly follows)*. I left a note on my pillow, grabbed a flashlight and quietly crept downstairs. When I opened the front door... It was...

RELIA. ...dark!

AURELIA. Country dark! *(RELIA leads, AURELIA follows as they begin "the journey.")* Bathed in moonlight, the windows of Granma's room stared down at me...like two dark eyes... I half expected her to call me back.

RELIA. She would shake me good for doing something so foolish!

AURELIA. But all was quiet... A deep breath and I was headed to Faison's. Every summer, when Granma said "Run down to Faison's and get a loaf of bread," ...like a flash, I was down this road and back. But now...

RELIA. It seemed to take forever...

AURELIA. And even in the moonlight... It was...

RELIA. ...so dark!

AURELIA. I passed the church graveyard...

RELIA *(whispers in fear)*. There's no such thing as ghosts... There's no such thing as... *(AURELIA and RELIA back into each other. Both are scared. RELIA screams and runs.)*

AURELIA. Faster and faster I ran... *(Lights of a passing car.)*

RELIA. Car!

AURELIA. Duck!

RELIA. Down! *(Car has passed.)* Let's go... *(Starts to run. Breathless:)* Made it!

AURELIA. Faison's was closed.

RELIA *(looking in store window)*. Must be after ten...

AURELIA. Main street... a ghost town...

RELIA *(whispering)*. "I don't believe in ghosts... I don't believe in..."

AURELIA. A fork in the road...

RELIA *(reading sign)*. Forty miles to... Turn left...

AURELIA *(taking flashlight and reading crossroads sign)*. Are you sure? *(Sound of a car on the highway. AURELIA and RELIA duck.)*

RELIA. The flashlight! *(RELIA turns flashlight off. BOTH crouch in the dark.)* It's gone... *(RELIA turns on flashlight and notices railroad tracks.)* Look! The railroad tracks! We could follow the tracks, that way we won't have to worry about cars passing.

AURELIA. But you don't know which way...

RELIA. As long as we can see the main road, we're fine! *(RELIA dashes for tracks.)*

AURELIA. Wait! *(AURELIA runs to catch up.)* By flashlight and moonlight, I hopped from tie to tie... There were shapes in the trees... shadowy figures moving in the mist... My stomach felt like a giant hole. *(Train whistle and train lights.)*

RELIA. Oh, God!

AURELIA. Huge cars almost sucked me back onto the tracks. *(Train sound and lights end.)* Squatting in the bushes in the after-silence... there were all kinds of sounds...

RELIA *(whispering)*. ... a cricket... an owl...

AURELIA. A cab driver's voice in the night... A child crying softly...

RELIA. What?

AURELIA. Nothing.

RELIA (*as animal runs across her feet*). AHHHHHHHHH!
(*RELIA jumps up.*)

AURELIA. Get back on the tracks! (*Frightened, BOTH try
to figure out what to do.*) What did they say in the workshop?

RELIA. Clear your mind.

AURELIA. Find something that gives you strength...

RELIA. That gives you courage...

AURELIA. For a while, I was Harriet Tubman, leading
slaves to freedom. I knew from Dad...

RELIA. Home was north, and a little bit west. Big Dipper,
Pointer Stars, Little Dipper...

AURELIA. I would have checked for moss on the north
side of a tree, but I didn't want to leave the tracks again.

AURELIA/RELIA. Big Dipper, Pointer Stars, Little Dipper...

RELIA. There! It's mine... Now it's my star, too! (*AURE-
LIA is briefly out of the moment, watching. She is sad.
She walks a few steps ahead of RELIA and is very quiet.
RELIA does not notice the change.*)

AURELIA. So why can't I find it?

RELIA. The tracks are going the right way. Come on.
We've got a long way to go.

AURELIA. To crowd out dark thoughts and dark skies.

RELIA. By the shores of Gitche Gumee...by the shining
Big Sea waters...

AURELIA. I recited all the poems and songs and stories I
learned in school.

RELIA. I used to wonder why they taught all that stuff.
Now, I know it's to fill odd moments, like this, when
you don't have anything important to think about.

AURELIA. I recited multiplication tables.

RELIA. 6 x 12 = 72... *(RELIA looks to AURELIA to answer.)*

AURELIA. I tried to figure out how many Bible verses I knew.

RELIA. One. Jesus wept. Two. In the beginning, God created the heaven and the earth... Three... *(Whispering softly with AURELIA.)* Suffer the little children to come... *(Sound of a very faint rumble of thunder in the distance.)*

AURELIA. I was glad I was not a stupid person and had studied well in school, otherwise, I would have been...

RELIA *(pause, frightened realization)*. Lost?

AURELIA. No matter how I strained, I couldn't see the main road.

RELIA. Oh, God! I know the road goes home...

AURELIA. But, I only *guessed* about the *tracks*. I had planned to follow them only as long as I could see the road. If I hadn't been playing stupid games...

RELIA. Oh, Lord! The North Star is gone! What do I do?

AURELIA. Go back!

RELIA. How far? If I lose too much time, I won't make it. *(Pause. Shines flashlight about.)* I'll cut cross the field and see if I can find the road.

AURELIA. No!

RELIA. It can't be too far. *(Begins to run.)*

AURELIA. No! *(RELIA does not stop.)* The field was muddy from last night's rain. The further I got from the track, the muddier it became.

RELIA *(panicking)*. Where's the road?

AURELIA. The more I walked, the more I believed...

RELIA *(slogging through mud)*. Just a few more steps... I'll find it.

AURELIA. My heart pounded... My mouth went dry... It was harder and harder to move in the sticky field. Red mud was past my ankles.

RELIA. A swamp! I'm in a swamp!

AURELIA. Stop! It's mud! *(A loud clap of thunder; lightning at the same time. RELIA and AURELIA scream. BOTH run. Rain pours... They must shout to hear. RELIA is running aimlessly. [Note: In her running, AURELIA can slip flashlight in her bag.])* The flashlight! I've lost the flashlight. Where's the flashlight? Where's the road! *(AURELIA tries to grab RELIA, but can't.)* Stop! Stop...

RELIA *(hysterical).* The North Star! Look for the... Oh, God... Oh, God. It's raining so hard! Where is it? Daddy, where is...

AURELIA *(grabs RELIA and is shaking her hysterically).* There is no stupid North Star. What the hell was I thinking... Could your precious North Star stop that stupid cab driver... Stop my daughter from hearing those words... Stop her tears... *(AURELIA/RELIA drop down in mud and cry in the rain.)*

RELIA *(hysterical and crying).* I found it, Daddy... I found it... I just couldn't hold onto it!

AURELIA. There is no North Star! It's just dark!

RELIA. Dark! *(Lights fade out.)*

SCENE FOUR

(Granma's house. GRANMA notices RELIA's light is still on.)

GRANMA. Relia, Relia... Turn off that light in there, girl! You too big to sleep with a light on! Waste of electricity. Relia? Relia! *(GRANMA picks up note.)* Oh my, God!

SCENE FIVE

(Aurelia's house. The same night. Around midnight. HAWKINS is banging on the door, frantically. MANSON and KATE have been asleep. MANSON goes to the door.)

HAWKINS *(off)*. Manson! Katie! Open up!

(MANSON opens door.)

MANSON. What's wrong?
HAWKINS. Your mother's been trying to get you for over an hour.

(KATE enters.)

KATE. What's wrong?
HAWKINS. The phone must have been off the hook.
KATE. We had to get some sleep.
MANSON. Man, what's wrong?

HAWKINS. It's Relia! She's run off!

KATE. What?

HAWKINS. You're mother said she left a note. She's trying to get here for the demonstration tomorrow.

KATE. What kind of crazy ...

MANSON. Doesn't matter. Kate, call Mama, try to find out what time she thinks Relia left. I'll get dressed... Kate! *(KATE tries to dial, but is confused. MANSON exits to bedroom. Returns with pants and shirt. Begins to dress as he listens.)*

HAWKINS. Your mother had a neighbor drive up the main route to Warren. She figured she couldn't have gotten much further than that. They didn't see her. She must not be on the main road. You think we should call the police?

MANSON. Oh, God. Ahhhhh. No... not yet. Not with what's happened to Willie. I don't want too many of them knowing she's out there. Oh, God!

HAWKINS. That's a smart little girl, you got, Manson. She'll be fine. She's got a lot of good sense.

KATE. It's been raining most all night...

MANSON. I'm going to drive straight out there. Go to the Reverend. Have him get some men together and four or five cars. Have one start a slow search from here, another about halfway and have at least Doc and whoever's with him come straight to my mother's and start there.

HAWKINS. You got it!

MANSON. Oh, tell them, no matter what— Call here, or my mama's every half hour or so. I don't care if they have to wake up every farmer in the county, just get to a phone.

HAWKINS. Right... What about Kate?

MANSON. Willie's here.

HAWKINS. I'm gone. *(HAWKINS exits.)*

KATE. Mama... Mama...

MANSON. Katie, let me speak... *(MANSON gently takes phone from KATE.)*

SCENE SIX

(A muddy field. RELIA and AURELIA sit side by side. They are wet and covered with mud. They are lost and in quiet shock.)

AURELIA. The rain was cold, but I stopped feeling it.

RELIA. How long have I been sitting in the mud?

AURELIA/RELIA. It's so dark...

AURELIA. I look at the sky and curse every star, every planet, every solar system that exists.

RELIA. I can't go back, 'cause I don't know which way to go...

AURELIA. And I can't go forward, 'cause I don't know which way to go...

AURELIA/RELIA. All I could think of was Daddy said...

RELIA. "When I needed it, I would find it."

AURELIA. But there is no North Star in the rain. No North Star... I don't know what to do? *(Pause.)*

RELIA. We'll do what Daddy said. We'll close our eyes, and count to a hundred. Our eyes will get used to the dark.

AURELIA. We've been out here for hours. Our eyes are already used to the dark...

RELIA. Then why are we so afraid?

AURELIA. It's not this dark. It's not this dark we're trying to fight. You'll close your eyes and they won't ever get used to...to...the... The dark we're trying to fight is hiding behind this night.

RELIA. What is it? You're frightening me. Is there something out there, something out there that will hurt me?

AURELIA. There's another kind of dark... You don't know about it yet...

RELIA. Let's count. Daddy says...

AURELIA. In this dark...there isn't any daddy... There's a frightened little girl but there isn't any daddy... There's nobody else... It's so vast... And there are no stars...

RELIA. Close your eyes. Close your eyes and count... You'll see... Count!

AURELIA. Why?

RELIA. What else is there to do? We must do something. We must do something, 'cause we've got to go on. So count. (*Pause.*) We'll count, and then at a hundred, we go on. No matter what, pick a direction and go. Close your eyes. One, two...three... Count!

AURELIA. It won't...

RELIA (*shouting, angry*). COUNT!

AURELIA (*closes eyes*). One, two, three...

SCENE SEVEN

(Granma's house. An hour later. GRANMA is on the phone.)

GRANMA. Manson, most everybody's checked in. The sheriff came by and got some of her clothes and a pair of shoes for the dogs. He's talked to all the police between here and there. A bunch of folks, white and black, have volunteered and are out looking. They're going house to house in each town. Manson. Go home. There are a lot of people out looking, somebody's going to find her. I talked to Kate. Just go home. Help with the phone calls. That's where you'll do the best good. Go home to Kate.

SCENE EIGHT

AURELIA/RELIA. Eighty-nine, ninety, ninety-one...

AURELIA. At first my eyes were closed so tightly, my head hurt.

RELIA. Find it here...

AURELIA. I watched the dark behind my eyelids...it was as infinite as the night sky. The more I counted, the more I relaxed. At about ninety-seven... I began to see...

RELIA. Dots?

AURELIA. Yeah, dots...dancing behind my lids...dots...

RELIA. Or maybe... *(They stand, eyes closed, but as if they can see something in front of them...slowly they begin to laugh. AURELIA and RELIA take each other's hands.)*

AURELIA/RELIA. Stars...?

AURELIA. Stars! Find it here!

RELIA. Stars in a night sky... They stopped dancing and I could make out patterns. Just like the ones in the book.

AURELIA. Patterns like Daddy had pointed out...

RELIA. There's Orion... and the Bear...

AURELIA. And the Pointer Stars... and... and... In the center of all those stars...

RELIA. Not the brightest...

AURELIA. But bright enough...

RELIA. I can see it... I can see it!

AURELIA/RELIA. The North Star!

RELIA. Now, all I have to do is open my eyes!

AURELIA. No! *(Pause.)*

RELIA. Once you've found it... you can find it again... *(RELIA takes AURELIA's hand. They open their eyes.)*

AURELIA. I remember now. When I opened my eyes, it was still dark...

RELIA. Not as dark...

AURELIA. I remember. When I opened my eyes... the rain came down gently. *(Pause.)*

RELIA. There was no light in the sky,

AURELIA. But when I opened my eyes... I still could see my North Star! *(Pause. Sound of thunder.)*

RELIA. Tomorrow's the demonstration! *(Thunder.)* We've got to get out of here! *(Lightning flashes.)*

AURELIA. Somebody's got to own this field. *(Lightning.)*

RELIA. Look, look over there!

AURELIA. I can't make anything out! *(In the next flash of light, RELIA sees a shape.)*

RELIA. Keep looking. Wait for the lightning flash... *(Flash.)*

AURELIA. Look! There! A barn!

RELIA. There's a barn over there...

AURELIA. I see it! I see it! It's gone.

RELIA. Come on! *(AURELIA and RELIA struggle, make it to the barn and collapse in the dark.)* Thank God! *(RELIA laughs as she realizes she is covered with mud.)* Lord, I look like Granma's pig.

(They laugh until they hear a dog barking. JAKE, a big white man with a lantern and a shotgun, enters. He has a blanket around his shoulders.)

JAKE. Shut up!... Shut up, dog. Git! Who's there?... Who's there?

AURELIA. I couldn't speak. The bottom of my stomach lurched. A black girl in the dark with a white man. If anything happened to me, my father would surely kill this man and then my father would be killed. The huge shape filled the barn door. I could see no way 'round him...

JAKE. What in the world... What you doing here? Can you speak, gal? What you doing here? *(AURELIA tries to run past JAKE. He grabs her.)* Hold on. Hold on. *(AURELIA bites JAKE's hand. JAKE slings her across barn.)* Oww...Damn you! You little... What you do that for? Ain't tryin' to hurt ya... Awww...you got teeth like Clara's old mule... Awww... Just sit there! *(JAKE tosses RELIA a blanket he has over his shoulders.)* Throw this 'round you 'fore you die of cold. Now listen, I'm not gonna hurt you. I got girls myself... But you can't go wanderin' round here in the dark in a storm like this. You running away? *(RELIA shakes her head.)* Then what you doin'? Answer me, girl.

RELIA. Got lost.

JAKE. Live far?

RELIA. Next county.

JAKE. You got folks? *(RELIA nods.)* They must be worried sick. Lord... Well, come on. Ain't got no phone, but get in the pickup. I'll take you home. Come on... I'm not gonna eat ya. Come on. *(RELIA and AURELIA hold each other without moving.)* Now listen, you're cold and wet and shivering. I wouldn't leave a dog out like this. I'm not gonna hurt you, but if you don't come with me, I'll have to go fetch the sheriff. I can't just leave you out here.

AURELIA. It was the sheriff that did nothing about Willie getting beat up.

RELIA. You take me straight home?

JAKE. Yeah. I take you straight home. Truck's outside. Come on... *(Dog begins to bark.)* Shut up, dog! Shut up! Won't hurt you. Just sounds mean. Go on.

AURELIA. I must have fallen asleep as soon as the truck started. The next thing I knew, I was home.

(Relia's house and porch. KATE and MANSON sit holding each other. They follow AURELIA's description of the moment. WILLIE waits on the steps.)

AURELIA. As we walked up to the front porch, it seemed like everything was in slow motion. I saw the hazy forms of my mother and father, suspended, through the screen. Mommy was sitting so still. Daddy was on one knee in front of her, with his arms around her. My mother's face looked like a frightened child's and his was so sad that I thought it might break. When they heard us, their heads turned at the same instant. They seemed like startled deer caught in somebody's headlights. I think that was the first time I ever saw them as people. He moved to open the screen. Her body was perfectly still, then she moved with the swiftness of a doe. My mother held me for a very long time and didn't say anything. After he saw to it I was all right, I could hear my father thanking the man over and over again. My mother just held on like she would never let me go. When she did, the man was gone.

KATE *(whispering)*. Thank God... Praise his name. Lord, have mercy... You could have been killed out there. Half the world was out looking for you. Are you all right... Are you all right? *(Nods.)* Why? *(MANSON shakes his head, as if this is not the time.)*

AURELIA. My father held me. He let go and she took my hand as if I was a little child, a child which I knew I was not anymore, or at least, not in the same way. Then I saw... *(They look at each other.)*

RELIA. Willie...

WILLIE. It's big freedom tomorrow.

AURELIA. My mother took me in and bathed me. I was too tired to protest. She put me in the bed, kissed me and I fell asleep before she turned off the lights.

(WILLIE has exited. MANSON hangs up phone and sits, yawning on the sofa. KATE returns to MANSON.)

MANSON. Is she all right?

KATE. Sound asleep. *(Pause.)* It's past five o'clock.

MANSON. Oh, God. I'm so tired. I got Willie home and called everybody I know to call and told them. I've got to get some sleep. *(Yawns, starts to rise.)* In exactly four hours we'll be at the demonstration.

KATE. You're not still...

MANSON. What do you mean?

KATE. It's just been... first Willie, now Relia...

MANSON. How does that change things?

KATE. I guess I didn't expect all those people, especially the whites, and even the sheriff...

MANSON. What are you saying?

KATE. It would be like a slap in the face to...

MANSON *(pause)*. Wait a minute, Kate... let's not get confused about all this? They're not animals. They're human just like us. And if one of their children was lost, I'd search just like I searched for Relia. But that doesn't change the fact that tomorrow, if I want a hamburger at Woolworth's, they're not going to see me as a father, or a husband, or a mortician, they're going to see one thing. This! *(Holds up his black hand.)*

KATE. I know... but...

MANSON. When Relia goes to sit at that lunch counter tomorrow, she'll know nothing has changed. Nothing will change, unless we change it.

KATE. Fine! Then let *us* change it. So far, it seems like only our children... Relia doesn't need to be there.

MANSON. How can you say that after what she went through tonight.

KATE. Just postpone it!

MANSON. Postpone it and then what? The sun comes up
and the sun goes down and I'm supposed to thank my
God I made it through one more day!

KATE. Yes!...with all your family living and breathing!
Yes!

MANSON (*pause*). Living and breathing... You know,
sometimes, when I'm working late, over there, I stare at
the bodies. If you stare hard enough, long enough, your
mind plays tricks on you. You imagine they're breathing. Sometimes I wonder which group I belong to. My
chest goes up and down, but there's...like a weight I've
got to get off. I've got to get it off or I'll suffocate and
die. Do you hear me? Die.

KATE. Just hold off for a day or two...

MANSON. Hold off? Kate, all my years, I done had him
standing on my chest. I can't take you standing there
too. We're going to do this thing. We're going to do it
tomorrow.

KATE. Then, I don't want Relia there.

MANSON. You've got to understand...

KATE. No, understand me! This "thing" is swallowing you
up! I can see it! The meetings, the planning, living on
the edge... But it's different for me.

MANSON. Kate...

KATE. You're fighting for the fight. I'm fighting for the
end. And it will end...it has to. Afterwards, I plan to
have a life! I don't want "race" to be my life!

MANSON. Whether you want it to be or not, it is your life.

KATE. No, it can't be! Not all of it!

MANSON. Listen...

KATE. No, you listen! Do you realize how much time we
spend talking about...thinking about...dreaming about...

race! Not about culture, or our history … but race! We sit down at the table for a meal, go for a drive in the country, have people over for cards … before the evening is over, it's "what da white folks done done now" … or "what black folks ought to do … " It sucks up so much of us … so much of you, there's not much left for me anymore …

MANSON. It's not going to last forever, but right now …

KATE. There must be a point when we finally arrive, when we get there! Someday we have got to be free or I'll go crazy. There's got to be a day when I can sit in a garden by my child or even my grandchildren and touch their hair and smile and breathe deep, and there is nobody standing on my chest, either! That's what I'm working for. Getting there so we can get on with life. God, I keep dreaming, we may be the first generation in this country to do that! To get on with life!

MANSON. I want that too …

KATE. Manson, I'm so tired …

MANSON. I know, baby …

KATE. So tired … but I can make the phone calls, cook the lunches, go to the meetings, I can do it, as long as I know that someday we'll arrive. And when we get there … I want Aurelia to be a whole person … I don't want her to have all the scares and the hurts that we've had. I don't want her bloodied and mangled and piecemealed … She has a chance to be a whole person … She and the children after her have a chance.

MANSON. Not if they don't know … not if they don't remember.

KATE. I don't want her to go, Manson. I don't want her to see … I don't …

(*MASON and KATE look up. RELIA is standing there. They don't know how long she has been listening.*)

AURELIA. Don't want her to...to hear...

RELIA. I've got to go, Mama.

KATE. I think you did enough going for one night.

RELIA. Mama...

KATE. Are you going to defy me, girl?

MANSON. Kate, don't make it any harder than it is for her.

KATE. Did you see that boy's face? Do you want Relia to come home looking like that? Or worse? It's one thing for us to be out there...but I only have one little girl, and as much as I love you, I'm not ready to sacrifice her.

MANSON. Sacrifice her to what? We're sacrificing her now...to lies... Trying to protect her with lies that everything's all right. In one breath we tell her she's as good as everybody and in the next breath we tell her she has to be twice as good to make it. But we both know that one day, all those lies and that intricate tunnel we build to get through one more day, one more week, one more year, one more lifetime...at one point or another, that tunnel will collapse in on us, bury us! Crush us. (*Pointing to chest.*) Crush us here! Could anything worse happen out there? Even if they killed her, she would at least die in the truth. I don't want my daughter pretending to be a cleaning woman just to sit in a damn library!

RELIA (*pause*). Mama...

MANSON. Sweetheart, I want you to have your time in the garden, and someday I want to stand all night, all night and watch the stars without having to run to a meeting. But life just isn't like that now, baby.

RELIA. Mama, I'm sorry about tonight. I know you were worried. I didn't mean to hurt you. I wouldn't hurt you for the world... I love you, Mama, but I got to go. *(Pause.)*

MANSON. Kate, she's saying she's got to do this. Give the girl credit, Kate, and give her her due.

KATE. I couldn't stop you if I wanted to, could I?

SCENE NINE

(AURELIA sits looking at the sky. She begins "Ain't Gonna Let Nobody Turn Me 'Round..." in the dark. The lights fade up on a tableaux of a lunch counter. The next day. We see fragments of a demonstration as the scene progresses. Some KKK hoods are visible. FRANKLIN, WILLIE, KATE, RELIA and MANSON enter. All other characters become the MOB VOICES, that jeer and spit.)

AURELIA. Next day, we slipped into our seats at Woolworth's. *(RELIA and AURELIA sit with MANSON.)*

MANSON. Keep your eyes straight ahead.

FRANKLIN. We'd like to be served.

MR. CONNELL. Not at my lunch counter...

AURELIA. In a seventeen-month boycott, my mother lasted one day. All agreed her temperament more suited driving people to shop in Raleigh during the boycott. But on that day, she was there... So was Willie...

RELIA. Face bruised...

WILLIE. Book, (*Pats pocket.*) candy bar, (*Pats another pocket and whispers.*) underwear! In case of arrest!

FRANKLIN. We sat for a while. Nothing happened.

AURELIA. One white woman I didn't know, smiled and whispered...

WOMAN (*from mob, in shadows*). You had quite a trip last night, didn't you, young lady?

AURELIA (*embarrassed*). Eyes down, I nodded. Then I heard Willie whisper...

WILLIE. It's them!

AURELIA. I wanted to turn around...

MANSON. Look straight ahead.

AURELIA. I heard them ...

CROWD VOICES. Hey! You!

AURELIA. It got louder...

CROWD VOICES. Hey, you! Jiggaboo!

AURELIA. I blanked out my mind and tried to think of something to fill it.

AURELIA/RELIA. ...number facts, [7 X 4 = 28] states, [Alabama, North Caroli...] countries, [Egypt, England] continents, [Africa...] Bible verses... [Jesus wept].

AURELIA. I closed my eyes and tried to see the stars just like I saw them last night...

RELIA. Big Dipper, Pointer Stars, Little Dipper, North Star...

AURELIA. I screamed them in my head to drown out what the crowd was saying...

RELIA. Big Dipper, Pointer Stars, Little Dipper, North Star...

CROWD VOICES. Hey, you, Nigger!

KATE. We need to go.

RELIA. Big Dipper... Little Dipper

KATE. Manson, we need to go... I don't want her to hear...

AURELIA. I don't want her to hear...

MANSON. No.

RELIA. Big Dipper, Pointer Stars, Little Dipper, North Star...

CROWD VOICES. Nigger!

AURELIA. I tried to block it out... but then someone screamed...

CROWD VOICES. Hey, you! I'm talking to you, NIGGER!!

KATE. Manson!

MANSON. Kate!

RELIA. North... North...

AURELIA. North... North... People had said the word before... I had heard...

CROWD VOICES. Nigger...

AURELIA. I knew they were talking about my race... but no one had ever called me...

CROWD VOICES *(whisper)*. Nigger!

AURELIA. I tried to block it out...

RELIA. Big... Dip... Point... Stars, Little... North ...

AURELIA. I tried, Big Dipper, Pointer Stars... North Star... I tried, but the word slipped by... It passed my ears and for the first time in my life... I *heard*... it!

CROWD VOICES. NIGGER! *(Darkness. We are aware only of AURELIA's upper body, and RELIA.)*

AURELIA. I couldn't see the face, but I could feel his thin, knife-sharp lips, carve away at the years my mother had protected me. The rasping, crazed edge in his voice did not cut cleanly, but made a flesh-ripping, jagged tear.

CROWD VOICES. Nigger...

AURELIA. I grabbed my heart and began to cry. I saw my mother's eyes and knew she knew.

CROWD VOICES. Nigger...

AURELIA. I was naked and wanted to cover my shame.

CROWD VOICES. Nigger..

AURELIA. I didn't want her to know. Because it would hurt her so. Because she could not patch the ragged flesh...

CROWD VOICES. Nigger!

AURELIA. So the wound became her wound and when the blood ran down from her heart, I could do nothing to stop her pain... She was naked before me as Eve before God.

RELIA. Mama... *(Sound of spitting is heard as FRANK-LIN, MANSON, KATE, and RELIA take turns wiping spit off the back of their necks.)*

AURELIA. This was different from yesterday's fear of being lost...fear of the night... It was the darker dark... Last night I was a little girl growing up. Today, I was a black girl growing up.

RELIA. I want to die.

AURELIA. There was a searing, knowing pain, but I could not die. I could only sit there, hand on my heart, hurting more with each breath. My mother knew... and then my father. There was no "I told you so" between them... Just their hands on my shoulder, squeezing as if they, together, could keep me from breaking. I must keep my child from breaking...

MANSON. Do you want to go?

AURELIA/RELIA. No.

RELIA. It hurt so badly.

AURELIA. I now understand the breach between my parents. My father felt the wound would heal and I would be stronger for it. My mother felt no wound at all best, and I would be freer for it. It was not an issue now. The wound was there and would not go away.

RELIA. We would never talk about it.

AURELIA. But I must tell my daughter. *(Long pause.)* When I turned around, I saw the man who brought me home in the storm.

(JAKE is surprised to see RELIA. He almost waves, but stops when he hears the crowd.)

AURELIA/RELIA. He was with the group spitting on us and yelling "Nigger" this and "Nigger" that. When he saw me, he froze, our eyes met, he almost smiled. The spit dribbled down his chin. When he wiped it away, he must have felt the eyes of his friends.

CROWD VOICES. Do you know her?

AURELIA/RELIA. He took a deep breath, called me "Nigger"... it sounded hollow, with no conviction. I almost felt sorry for him when he grabbed his heart. *(Pause.)* Then he spit right in my face...

WILLIE. Noooooo... *(WILLIE jumps up to attack JAKE. RELIA stops him.)*

RELIA. Ice water!

AURELIA. Willie wanted to kill him but I gritted my teeth and whispered...

RELIA. "Ice water!" *(WILLIE lunges again.)* "Ice Water!"... Remember, Willie. Don't let a glass of ice water defeat you, Willie. *(WILLIE doesn't back off.)* That's a little freedom, Willie. We're working for the big freedom, now...

WILLIE *(begins to pull back)*. The big freedom...

RELIA. Shines like a star! *(A VOICE begins singing softly "Ain't Gonna Let Nobody Turn Me 'Round...")*

AURELIA/RELIA.
I shall not want...

WILLIE.
To kill... *(Pause. He sits.)*

He maketh me lie down in

KATE.
green gardens...

RELIA.
The big freedom

VOICES/WILLIE.
He restoreth my soul...

Stronger than evil.

KATE.
How deep the scar

AURELIA.
But the wound begins to heal...

I must tell my daughter...

Though I walk through the valley of the shadow of death...

RELIA.
Love overcomes hate...

AURELIA.
Climb on up to higher ground...

I shall fear no evil.

WILLIE.
For thou art with me.

RELIA.
Spit swear!

VOICES/WILLIE.
In the presence of my enemies...
Restoreth my soul... *(Pause.)*

AURELIA/RELIA.
Find it here!
See millions and millions of stars...

AURELIA. I never saw the man there again...

(ALL sing "Ain't Gonna Let Nobody Turn Me 'Round..."
KATE holds RELIA. ALL take a moment to look at the
sky before exiting. Song continues softly as they each
leave while looking up at the stars. AURELIA, RELIA
and MANSON are left on stage.)

AURELIA. Demonstrations and boycotts continued for
months. After things cooled off a bit, Willie quietly got
his job back at the *integrated* library. Mama was right. It
wasn't all over in a day or a month or a summer...
(Dark sky with brilliant stars fade up as AURELIA
speaks.) I would fight again and again, until I lost the
glimmer of a star in my heart among all those tall,
brightly lit buildings. The stars are faint in the sky
above—but they are there. And I don't walk in the dark
very much anymore, unless forced to. It's too dangerous
here. But, I know tonight, before I turn out the lamp, I
must tell my daughter... "There will be no school tomorrow." Our school will be at the Grand Cab Company and
I will be the teacher. And tonight, before I turn out the
lamp, I will hold my daughter close...and show her my
scars. I will weep with her and let my tears wash her
wounds. I will pray for her children and her children's
children, then dry her face and tell her to close her eyes.
"Look up. There's a whole universe of light inside us!
We just have to find it." *(RELIA and MANSON watch*
the stars.)

RELIA. Look up! See!

MANSON. A whole universe of stars!

AURELIA. There really is a North Star...

MANSON. And if you find it once, you can find it again.
AURELIA. Turn off the lights... *(Slowly begins counting as lights fade.)*
AURELIA/RELIA. One, two, three... *(Lights fade to darkness except for stars and a very bright light on AURELIA, as if she is a star. She touches her heart, as if pained, looks up, smiles when she sees the North Star.)*
RELIA *(points to the sky)*. There!
AURELIA *(points to her heart)*. Here!

THE END

PRODUCTION NOTES

SET: Consists of multiple levels which can transform into a variety of playing spaces. Key areas are Relia's front porch and house, the library, the funeral parlor (optional), church, church basement, Granma's house, a dark country road, barn, the eating counter of a southern department store, and a city beach. Aurelia is constantly on stage. Though ever present, she will need spaces to observe from while other scenes, which don't directly include her, occur. For convenience, the play is broken up into acts/scenes, but in most cases the scenes should flow from one to the next like a story, without pause.

Costumes, lights and sounds should be simple and suggest the fluidity of memory.

The sky, in many forms, is a constant presence.

DIRECTOR'S NOTES